Praise for *Artificial Intelli*
in the Primary Classrc

This text provides a plethora of activities and insights into how artificial intelligence can be utilised positively to support learning, reduce teacher workload, and inspire pupils in our primary classrooms.

It will be especially useful for educators who are feeling anxious about adopting artificial intelligence into their teaching, as Gemma Clark helps explain how to use AI in an accessible and purposeful way, thereby removing the fear of this new technology and instead fostering excitement and inspiration.

All primary curriculum subject areas are covered, as well as a wide range of extracurricular areas where AI can be employed, such as in outdoor learning spaces, in assemblies, and even in after-school clubs.

An inclusive approach is carefully considered in this text, with specific chapters exploring how AI can support pupil well-being, staff well-being, and learners, including those who are neurodivergent.

If you haven't considered how AI can reduce your teacher workload, aid personalised learning, and help you to restore a more comfortable work–life balance, then this is the book for you!

Dr Poppy Gibson, Course Lead and Senior Lecturer in Primary Education,
Anglia Ruskin University

Gemma's insightful book on AI has played a crucial role in helping me overcome the initial uncertainty and confusion surrounding the topic. It has not only provided me with valuable guidance and ideas, but has also instilled in me the much-needed confidence to delve into the world of AI. Thanks to Gemma's book, I now understand the practicality and potential impact of AI, demonstrated by my use of AI to compose this response.

Toria Bono, teacher, leader, and author of
Tiny Voices Talk: Education, Engagement, Empowerment

In a landscape where education constantly evolves to meet the demands of the digital age, Gemma's latest book stands out as a beacon of innovation and inspiration for teachers and school leaders, venturing as it does into the realm of artificial intelligence in the primary classroom. Important to state at the outset, this is not a book full of lesson plans; rather, it is an extremely helpful tool to help you start to visualise how to constructively incorporate AI into your daily teaching and planning.

The great strength of this book is the sheer diversity of topics and issues it covers in a simple format. From how to incorporate AI into curricular areas such as literacy, maths, science and art, to how to develop schoolwide policies on mobile phone usage or implementing effective behaviour management strategies. This book is a must-use guide to bring your classroom and school in line with 21st century technology and thrive using it.

There is currently a feeling among educators and others that using AI to help in the planning of teaching is somehow cheating or challenging our professionalism. This is a viewpoint that needs to change, and this guide is an ideal tool to help make that shift in our mindset to one that embraces innovation.

As a primary teacher herself, Gemma writes with humour and a full understanding of what your day-to-day job entails, helping to provide practical tips on every page to address the challenges of teaching today. What is hugely commendable is her embedding of inclusive practice throughout the book – especially for EAL learners, neurodiverse learners, and teachers – and decolonising practices. All current and important issues.

Gemma also highlights how using AI in the classroom can be a way to model its use in a positive way for learners. AI is not going anywhere, but incorporating it into pupil research, for instance, will help learners to understand that it is not about trying to find the answers, but is about helping them to ask critical questions and delve deeper into their learning.

As Gemma states, 'We stand at the threshold of a new technological revolution'. We therefore simply must embrace the advancements in technology and I recommend starting with this book as an excellent step forward.

Nuzhat Uthmani, Lecturer in Primary Education at the University of Stirling, Founder of Global Citizenship Education in Scotland Ltd

Gemma Clark

Artificial Intelligence
in the
Primary Classroom

ways to save time, cut your workload and enhance your creativity

Crown House Publishing Limited

www.crownhouse.co.uk

First published by

Crown House Publishing Limited
Crown Buildings, Bancyfelin, Carmarthen, Wales, SA33 5ND, UK
www.crownhouse.co.uk

and

Crown House Publishing Company LLC
PO Box 2223, Williston, VT 05495, USA
www.crownhousepublishing.com

First published 2024.

British Library Cataloguing-in-Publication Data

A catalogue entry for this book is available from the British Library.

Print ISBN 978-178583714-2
Mobi ISBN 978-178583715-9
ePub ISBN 978-178583716-6
ePDF ISBN 978-178583717-3

LCCN 2023947862

Printed and bound in the UK by
TJ Books, Padstow, Cornwall

To my husband, the love of my life, and my mum, who has always encouraged my education and my writing. I am forever grateful to have you both in my life.

Foreword

Artificial intelligence is not going to change the world; it's already changing it. Right now, someone is using AI to analyse X-rays and speed up diagnoses. Someone else is using an AI chatbot to activate a credit card. Phones are being unlocked using AI algorithms. AI is being used to prevent fraud and deployed to sift through military data. Whether you're directly aware of it or not, AI is everywhere.

All technological developments can be daunting, and shifts on the scale that we're about to witness sometimes produce particularly acute anxieties. These fears are not unfounded, and it's entirely possible that the introduction of AI to education – if driven by the wrong people or pursued for the wrong purposes – could be hugely damaging.

It's not difficult to imagine a spreadsheet-worshipping bureaucrat in a council office deploying AI for the purposes of tracking and monitoring, or decreeing that all teachers must produce lessons plans aligned to an AI-generated template. Someone, somewhere, is calculating how much money they can save by having AI calculate how much money they can save. The risks are real.

Like any technology, there's enormous potential for misuse, and the sheer scale of AI's possibilities means that concerns over its inevitable creep into education are entirely reasonable. Teachers are, sadly, well used to being told that they just need to make things work while being given little if any support.

There will be some who think the best approach is to resist – as far and for as long as possible – the adoption of this new, immensely powerful but potentially destructive technology. That's an entirely understandable response, but ignorance isn't bliss, progress can't be halted, and there's nothing to be gained from pretending that schools can be isolated from broader societal shifts.

The tide is rising no matter what we do, and planting our feet in the same point in the sand only ends one way. If teachers – or any number of other professionals – try to ignore AI, they will, in the end, find themselves overwhelmed by it when their makeshift levees inevitably break.

But that is where books like this one might come in. For Gemma Clark, AI is not the enemy – it is a potential ally. Specifically, she believes that it might be a tool to help address the workload crisis that has been engulfing the profession for years. That is, of course, a problem that can't be solved by teacher innovation alone, and it's always important not to let politicians and other decision-makers off the hook. However, if we can make machines do at least some of the bureaucratic and organisational leg-work involved in teaching, maybe that could free up teachers to spend more time doing what they want to be doing, and what we need them to be doing? Maybe if AI is applied well, teachers could get on with teaching?

This book feels like a potentially important step in that direction. Some of the suggestions, like the use of AI to generate lists of spelling words, are relatively simple; others, such as deploying this new technology to summarise lengthy documents full of government guidance, speak to more fundamental changes in behaviour. As a former English teacher, ideas like using an AI image generator to develop students' writing skills are particularly intriguing. Crucially, all are presented with a view to freeing up teachers to spend more time on the stuff that a computer, no matter how much artificial intelligence is poured into it, cannot do.

James McEnaney, journalist and author

Contents

Contents

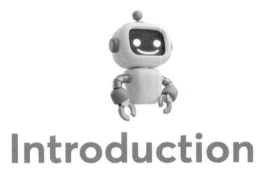

Introduction

Artificial intelligence (AI) undoubtedly sparks debate among teachers. Questions arise about the trajectory of this new technology: where will it take us? How will we differentiate between pupil-authored work and AI-generated content? What impact will it have on the dynamics of learning and teaching within schools? Will it lead to a loss of creativity and critical thinking skills? These are all crucial topics for discussion. Yet, AI has already become part of our reality, and I firmly believe that embracing its potential is in our best interests.

I understand first hand the challenges posed by our bureaucracy-heavy profession and its demanding workload. While I may not possess an inherent aptitude for technology or the ability to effortlessly implement technological solutions, I have identified 101 ways through which AI can alleviate this burden. There is a plethora of accessible AI mobile apps and free online platforms to choose from, such as Adobe Firefly and ChatGPT; even Snapchat has added a decent AI bot to the app, My AI.

These approaches not only restore a semblance of work–life balance by streamlining routine tasks and providing simple solutions that save time, AI also enables us to redirect our focus towards the important job of nurturing young minds, targeting our energy and resources into higher impact activities, such as creating tailored learning experiences, giving children personalised feedback, and improving engagement. It can also help us to tap into our creative reserves and make full use of the resources we already have available. Beware of Americanised spelling; however, you can always ask it to use English spelling.

AI has the capacity to revolutionise the teaching profession. We don't need to meet this paradigm shift with trepidation; rather, we should welcome it as a long-awaited remedy to our workload conundrum.

1. Spelling Lessons

AI can streamline your spelling lesson planning process, ultimately saving you valuable time. For instance, by inputting a simple query such as, 'Provide me with eight lengthy words containing "oi",' an AI bot can produce a list within seconds, which you can easily copy and paste into your materials.

You could then enter the instruction, 'Generate eight moderately simpler words' and, just like that, differentiation becomes an effortless task. In a matter of moments, AI can create three tailored word lists, each suited to a different level of difficulty. I typed 'Offer me eight four-letter words with "oi"' and the AI app provided the following graded examples:

1	coincidence	soil	coin
2	moisturiser	oil	boil
3	exploiters	foil	soil
4	recoiling	toil	join
5	embroidery	coil	moil
6	turquoise	spoil	roil
7	poisoning	broil	toil
8	rejoicing	recoil	void

So, what if you find yourself in a situation where you are a new teacher or at a school without a specific spelling programme, and the teachers are essentially self-navigating through the challenges (we have all been there)? Not to worry! Just turn to AI and request a list of phonemes or 'sounds suitable for teaching young children', and watch as the app promptly devises a comprehensive list for you.

2. Writing resources

As a teacher who is passionate about teaching writing, I have found AI to be an exciting resource. It can save considerable time in the process of differentiated planning, affording me more time to create imaginative writing prompts. For instance, if I want to dedicate time to painting eggs with gold paint to simulate the presence of a magical dragon visiting the classroom overnight, I have that flexibility because I have had to spend less time on more mundane tasks!

AI apps can be harnessed to rapidly generate useful writing resources like sentence openers and vocabulary. Typing 'Give me 10 adjectives to describe a magic dragon' returns:

1 Majestic

2 Enchanting

3 Radiant

4 Mysterious

5 Fierce

6 Resplendent

7 Bewitching

8 Awe-inspiring

9 Ethereal

10 Legendary

Or, for different kinds of writing, AI can quickly give you eight persuasive sentence openers – for example:

1 Imagine a world where …

2 Did you know that …?

3 Picture this …

4 Have you ever considered …?

5 It's time to take action and …

6 Are you ready to ...?

7 In today's fast-paced world, it is crucial to ...

8 You deserve to experience ...

You can even request very specific sentence openers such as 'ly' openers:

1 Interestingly, ...

2 Clearly, ...

3 Surprisingly, ...

4 Fortunately, ...

5 Interestingly enough, ...

6 Undoubtedly, ...

7 Strikingly, ...

8 Importantly, ...

All of this gives you more time to spend on the fun stuff.

3. AI Images for Story Prompts and Creativity

Using AI-generated images as a creative tool for story writing prompts can be fun for the children. For instance, you could request an image of 'a haunted house with bats flying around' or 'a depiction of an enchanted forest'. This approach offers excellent opportunities to provide pupils with choices and individualisation during their writing lessons. If the children have access to tablets, the initial step of their writing task could involve generating an image of a setting on which they would like to base their writing. This exercise enables them to observe how particular words evoke distinct mental images, encouraging them to consider how language can enhance their descriptions.

This activity is not only engaging and enjoyable for children, but it also challenges them to develop a vocabulary that effectively conjures the imagery they imagine. Moreover, if the image produced doesn't align with their vision, it can prompt them to consider how to communicate their preferences better to the AI app.

We have all encountered some amusing and/or peculiar AI-generated images, so we know this experience can be effective in sparking the children's imagination. For instance, an image of a frog on a flying submarine might just be the catalyst for igniting a creative storytelling spark! As the teacher, you might use ICT time to get the children creating their own images or you may want to produce a specific image that fits your writing lesson objectives and display it to the whole class.

4. Reading Comprehension

As a child with undiagnosed dyslexia, I enjoyed reading, but I detested comprehension exercises. (I now realise this was due to the considerable amount of mental effort it demanded.) As a teacher, I observe that many pupils aren't enthusiastic about reading comprehension either. Nevertheless, it is a crucial skill and necessary for their educational advancement.

Since piquing the children's interest constitutes a significant portion of the challenge in most classrooms, imagine the possibility of orienting reading comprehension exercises towards subjects that resonate with a class or even with individual children. Thanks to AI, this has become an effortlessly achievable reality!

I recall a pupil with whom I struggled to foster engagement unless the content was customised to revolve around his interests in dinosaurs or minibeasts. AI could have swiftly provided me with a reading passage on centipedes, complete with accompanying questions and answers. Consequently, I could have presented this child with a reading task that he would have gladly embraced, and which would have spared me from dedicating hours to locating or crafting such materials myself.

Here is an example. 'Give me a passage about centipedes for a 7-year-old' generates:

Centipedes: Lots of Legs and Little Hunters

Centipedes are small creatures with lots and lots of legs! They are like mini superheroes in the bug world. Imagine having so many legs to walk with – it must be like wearing many pairs of shoes all at once!

These tiny creatures live in dark and damp places, like under rocks and leaves. They like to hide because they are a bit shy. When the sun goes down and it gets dark, they come out to explore and find their dinner.

Guess what they like to eat? Other bugs! Centipedes are great hunters. They use their special curved jaws to catch spiders, worms, and insects, even ants. They are like sneaky ninjas of the bug world, silently creeping up on their prey.

But don't worry, most centipedes won't bother humans. They are more interested in finding their bug-sized snacks. So, if you ever spot a centipede,

remember to give them some space – they are just busy looking for their
next meal!

The input, 'Give me five comprehension questions based on the above' suggests:

1   What is it like for centipedes to move with so many legs?
2   Where do centipedes like to live?
3   When do centipedes come out to explore?
4   What do centipedes like to eat?
5   Should you be afraid of most centipedes? Why or why not?

This list can be further individualised if you wish to focus on literal questions or inferential questions. It would take me less than a minute to copy and paste the above text
and questions into a document, ready for my pupil who would benefit from individualised tasks.

5. Poetry

AI has a lot of potential for poetry, whether it is creating poems to fit learning themes or generating examples of different kinds of poetry. You can be very specific.

Prompt: 'Write a child-friendly rhyming couplet poem about a butterfly'.

In fields of flowers, oh so spry,
A butterfly flits by the sky.
Its wings a rainbow, colours bright,
Dancing in the golden light.
With grace it lands on petals fair,
Spreading magic through the air.
Fluttering, it's a joyful sprite,
A painted wonder taking flight.

Or 'Write a poem in Scots language about a beloved pet cat'.

Ma braw wee pet, sae dear tae me,
A furry freend, aye blythe and free.
Wi' waggin' tail and sparklin' e'e,
Ye fill oor days wi' sic glee.
Ye loup and play, a bonnie sight,
Lichtin' up the gloomy night.
Nae maitter rain nor sun sae bricht,
Ye bring me joy wi' a' yer might.
Thro' fields we wander, hand in paw,
A bond sae true, nae flaw nor flaw.
Ye understand me, nane else saw,
My loyal freend, fore'er we'll draw.
Noo restin' in yer cozy bed,
I stroke yer fur, a gentle tread.

> Wi' love that niver fadeth, spread,
>
> My beloved pet, ye're a treasure, bred.

And, of course, AI can help you to plan a poetry lesson – for example, 'Plan a limerick writing lesson for 10-year-olds':

Limerick Writing for 10-Year-Olds

Objective: To introduce 10-year-old pupils to the concept of limericks and guide them in creating their own limerick poems.

Duration: 1–2 class periods (adjustable based on pace)

Materials:

- Whiteboard or chart paper
- Marker pens
- Limerick examples (written or printed)
- Lined paper or notebooks for pupils

Lesson steps:

1 Introduction to limericks:

- Begin by asking pupils if they have heard of limericks before. Share that limericks are fun and silly poems with a specific rhyme and rhythm pattern.
- Display or share examples of limericks. Read a few aloud to the class, emphasising the rhyme scheme and rhythm.

2 Rhyme and rhythm pattern:

- Discuss the AABBA rhyme scheme of a limerick, where the first, second, and fifth lines rhyme with each other, and the third and fourth lines rhyme with each other.
- Talk about the rhythm of a limerick, which is typically anapestic (da-da-DUM). Demonstrate the rhythm by clapping the syllables of a limerick line.

3 Brainstorming ideas:

- Engage pupils in a brainstorming session. Ask them for ideas on different topics they could use for their limericks. Encourage creativity and silliness!

- Write down some of their ideas on the whiteboard or chart paper for reference.

4 Writing limericks:

- Choose a topic from the brainstorming session as a class. Let's say the topic is 'pizza'.

- Together, construct a limerick using the AABBA rhyme scheme and the anapestic rhythm. Write the limerick on the board as you create it together.

- Explain that the limerick should have a funny or surprising twist in the last line. Encourage pupils to think of unexpected endings.

5 Independent writing:

- Distribute lined paper or notebooks to pupils.

- Instruct pupils to choose their own topic from the brainstorming session and start crafting their limericks. Remind them to focus on rhyme, rhythm, and the twist in the last line.

6 Sharing and feedback:

- Once pupils have completed their limericks, provide an opportunity for volunteers to share their poems with the class.

- Encourage positive feedback from peers. Discuss what makes a limerick funny and effective.

7 Limerick gallery:

- Collect the limericks from the pupils and create a limerick gallery display in the classroom.

- Invite pupils to read each other's limericks and appreciate the creativity and humour.

Extension:

- Challenge advanced pupils to create longer limerick chains, where each limerick's last line becomes the topic for the next limerick.

Assessment:

- Assess pupils' understanding of limericks based on their ability to adhere to the rhyme and rhythm pattern, create a twist in the last line, and produce a limerick that is entertaining and humorous.

By the end of this lesson, 10-year-old pupils should have a grasp of limerick structure and be able to write their own amusing limerick poems.

I find AI to be a very useful tool for teaching poetry across a range of genres.

6. Generating Cloze Procedures

Cloze procedures are educational tools used to assess and enhance reading comprehension skills, particularly in the context of language learning and literacy development. The technique involves presenting a passage of text with specific words or phrases removed. The reader is required to fill in the missing words based on the context and their understanding of the text. This approach encourages readers to actively engage with the text, infer meanings, and utilise their background knowledge to complete the gaps.

Missing word cloze procedures are commonly used in primary settings and can prove valuable in reinforcing what the children are learning in other curricular areas. However, it can take a significant amount of time to locate suitable passages or create them from scratch. Once again, AI can produce these passages within seconds and allow easy customisation to match individual interests and needs.

For example, 'Write a missing answer cloze procedure about the water cycle with answers included' generates:

The Water Cycle

The water cycle, also known as the hydrological cycle, is the continuous process by which water moves through the Earth's atmosphere and its surface. This cycle plays a crucial role in maintaining the Earth's water supply and regulating its climate. The water cycle consists of several key stages:

1 Evaporation is the process by which water from oceans, lakes, and rivers turns into water vapour due to the heat of the sun. The sun's energy causes the water to evaporate and rise into the _____.

2 As the water vapour rises higher into the atmosphere, it cools down and changes back into tiny water _____. The condensation causes clouds to form.

3 When the clouds become heavy and saturated with water droplets, the water falls back to the Earth's surface as _____. It can be in the form of rain, snow, sleet, or hail.

4 Some of the precipitation flows along the Earth's surface and collects in rivers, lakes, and oceans. This is known as runoff. It _____ the water bodies and continues the cycle.

5　Some of the precipitation seeps into the ground, a process known as
＿＿＿＿＿. This water can be stored in underground reservoirs called
aquifers.

6　Transpiration is the process by which plants absorb water through their
roots and release water vapour through tiny ＿＿＿＿＿ in their leaves. This
adds water vapour to the atmosphere.

The water cycle is a continuous and interconnected process that ensures the
availability of water for various living organisms and natural systems on
Earth.

Answers:

1　Atmosphere

2　Droplets

3　Precipitation

4　Replenishes

5　Infiltration

6　Pores

This comprehension activity can be copied and pasted into a document in seconds,
saving hours of your time.

7. Acrostic Poems

While there is much more to poetry than acrostic poems, I am sure we all agree that these are a great activity for getting children to think about vocabulary. AI can very quickly devise differentiated examples of acrostic poems for you to show the class – for example, you could challenge some children to use the word 'ghost' and more advanced learners to use the word 'Halloween' when they write their own acrostic poems.

Prompt: 'Write an acrostic poem for children using the word "Halloween".'

Hats and costumes, fun to wear,

A spooky night with a chilling air.

Laughter echoes, as pumpkins gleam,

Lanterns light up this Halloween dream.

Onward we go, into the night's embrace.

Witches and ghosts under moonlit skies.

Everyone's dressed in their favourite guise,

Eerie tales told with a shiver and cheer,

Nights like this are filled with delight!

Prompt: 'Write an acrostic poem for children using the word "ghost".'

Glowing white, they softly float,

Hiding in the shadows, a spectral gloat.

On misty nights, they appear to play,

Shadowy figures, here they stay.

Transparent beings, mysterious and shy.

8. Mystery Reading Challenges

Most children find mysteries more fun than traditional comprehension passages, and if there are clues to solve too, then more reluctant readers are more likely to engage. Nevertheless, they are all still having to understand and think about what they have read.

Prompt: 'Create a child-friendly mystery story about a stolen diamond. Ensure there are clues for children to work out who the thief is. Provide the thief's name at the bottom of the story so that it can be told to the children later.'

The Enchanted Diamond Mystery

In the magical land of Gemlandia, preparations were underway for the enchanting Gem Carnival. The crown jewel of the carnival was the dazzling Enchanted Diamond, a gem that radiated colours like a rainbow. The diamond was showcased inside a magnificent glass dome at the heart of the carnival.

Families and children flocked to the carnival, thrilled by the sight of sparkling gems. Among them were Lily and Max, two curious and clever friends. Their excitement turned into astonishment when a gasp swept through the crowd – the Enchanted Diamond had vanished!

Concern spread, and the organisers quickly summoned Detective Ruby, a wise and friendly fox known for solving the trickiest mysteries. She explained that the diamond had been stolen, and they needed to unravel the puzzle before the carnival came to an end.

Determined to help, Lily and Max joined forces with Detective Ruby. They interviewed witnesses, examined the scene, and discovered that three individuals had been near the diamond's display: Mr Goldstone, the jeweller; Madame Amara, the illusionist; and Professor Crystal, the gem expert.

Each suspect had their own story to tell. Mr Goldstone claimed to have been polishing a gem necklace, Madame Amara was practising her magic tricks, and Professor Crystal had been presenting a lecture about rare gems.

The young detectives pooled their observations and formed a theory. Max recalled reading that diamonds have unique qualities when exposed to light. Lily thought that a thief might have used light to their advantage.

They revisited Madame Amara and enquired about her magic tricks. She hesitated but then admitted that during her performance, she saw a sudden gleam of light that blinded her momentarily.

Armed with this new clue, they approached the suspects again. Professor Crystal confessed to accidentally directing sunlight with his magnifying glass, but he insisted he was innocent.

Mr Goldstone admitted to briefly leaving the diamond's case unlocked, but he denied any involvement in the theft.

Lily pieced together the facts and realised that the blinding light held the key. She gathered everyone at the carnival and explained that the light had been a clever distraction. The thief must have taken advantage of the moment and seized the diamond.

As Detective Ruby announced that they were close to solving the case, the carnival visitors applauded the young detectives. Detective Ruby thanked Lily and Max for their sharp insights.

And so, the young detectives continued to work together, gathering more clues and piecing together the puzzle of the Enchanted Diamond. Who was the thief? The answer awaits!

[The thief's name: Mr Goldstone]

Feel free to share the thief's name with the children, allowing them to connect the dots and celebrate their detective skills!

You can alter the mystery story in many ways by simply inputting, for example, 'Can you make the above Halloween themed?'

The Spooky Diamond Caper

In the eerie town of Hauntville, the air was filled with excitement as the annual Halloween Spectacle drew near. The main attraction of the event was the mysterious Shadowstone Diamond, a gem that shimmered like a phantom's glow. The diamond was displayed inside a grand, spiderweb-covered glass case at the heart of the spook-tacular event.

Families and kids roamed the streets, dressed in their Halloween costumes, eagerly anticipating the array of creepy delights. Among the crowd were siblings Mia and Ethan, a pair of sharp and adventurous detectives. Their excitement turned to intrigue when a collective gasp echoed – the Shadowstone Diamond had vanished!

Anxiety spread, and the event organisers called upon Detective Luna, a clever and friendly black cat known for solving perplexing mysteries. She explained that the diamond had been stolen, and they had to piece together the puzzle before the Halloween Spectacle reached its chilling end.

Eager to assist, Mia and Ethan teamed up with Detective Luna. They interviewed witnesses, examined the scene, and identified three suspects who were near the diamond's eerie display: Mr Ravenwood, the jeweller; Madame Morgana, the fortune teller; and Professor Cursedale, the gem historian.

Each suspect had a tale to share. Mr Ravenwood insisted he had been inspecting a haunted necklace, Madame Morgana was practising her mystical readings, and Professor Cursedale had been giving a talk about cursed gems.

Pooling their thoughts, the young detectives formulated a theory. Ethan recollected a story about diamonds changing colours when exposed to unique light. Mia suggested that the thief might have used a flash of light to their advantage.

They revisited Madame Morgana and enquired about her fortune-telling tricks. She hesitated, then revealed that during her performance, a sudden blinding flash of light momentarily obscured her vision.

Armed with this newfound clue, they returned to the suspects. Professor Cursedale admitted to accidentally reflecting moonlight with his magnifying glass, but he vehemently denied any involvement in the theft.

Mr Ravenwood confessed to momentarily leaving the diamond's case unlocked, but he maintained that he had not stolen it.

Mia connected the dots and realised the significance of the blinding light. Gathering everyone at the Halloween Spectacle, she explained that the flash had been a clever trick, designed to divert attention while the thief snatched the diamond.

With Detective Luna's assurance that they were close to solving the case, the Halloween crowd cheered for the young detectives. Detective Luna thanked Mia and Ethan for their sharp instincts.

The Halloween Spectacle continued, and the young detectives worked together to gather more clues, piecing together the enigma of the Shadowstone Diamond. Who was the thief? The answer is just around the corner!

[The thief's name: Mr Ravenwood]

9. Character Creation and Story Building

AI can serve as a playful and engaging tool for children to craft their own characters for writing lessons. For instance, children can request an AI image generator to produce a 'furry blue monster', which they can then describe in their narratives. AI can also aid them in producing descriptive settings which they can use as the basis for an imaginative story. The potential to elevate the writing experience while fostering engagement knows no bounds!

You could also input the images crafted by the children into an image-to-text converter, which would result in the generation of descriptive passages. This would not only provide the children with examples to read but also help them to explore and develop new vocabulary.

10. Fun and Magical Letters to Your Class

Utilising the magic of Easter bunnies, Father Christmas, or fun fictional characters can be a great hook for learning and engagement with young classes. For example, perhaps you want your class to write a persuasive letter. Wouldn't it help if they received an exciting letter from Father Christmas to which they could craft a reply?

Prompt: 'Write a letter from Father Christmas to a class saying that he is thinking of sending them a magic elf, but he is unsure and can the children write back telling him the reasons why they should have an elf.'

[Your Address]

[Street, City, Post Code]

[Date]

Dear [Teacher's Name] and [Class Name],

Greetings from the North Pole! I hope this letter finds you all in good spirits and excited for the festive season ahead. As I prepare for another wonderful Christmas, I wanted to take a moment to reach out to you, my dear friends from [Class Name].

You see, I've been pondering a delightful idea this year, one that involves a sprinkle of enchantment and a touch of magic. I've been thinking about sending one of my trusty magic elves to your classroom, but I find myself at a crossroads – a crossroads of excitement and wonder!

Now, my dear friends, this decision isn't an easy one for me. Elves are extraordinary creatures who bring laughter, joy, and a touch of mischief wherever they go. They have a way of making even the most ordinary days feel extraordinary. But I've been wondering: why should I send a magic elf to [Class Name]? What makes your class the perfect place for such a magical companion?

This is where you come in! I'd love to hear from each and every one of you about why you think your classroom should be the home of a mischievous and delightful magic elf. Do you have a heart-warming reason? A special holiday tradition? A creative idea for how the magic elf could spread holiday cheer? Share your thoughts with me!

You can write me a letter and let me know why you believe a magic elf would be a fantastic addition to your classroom. Feel free to include your wishes, dreams, and even a little hint of the holiday spirit. Once I've read all your wonderful letters, I'll make my decision with your heart-warming words in mind.

Remember, my dear friends, the holiday season is a time of togetherness, kindness, and the magic of believing. Whether or not a magic elf joins you, I am grateful for your warmth and excitement, and I wish you all a holiday season filled with laughter, love, and cherished memories.

Please send your letters to my special address at the North Pole by [Deadline Date]. I can't wait to read your heartfelt words and learn why [Class Name] is the perfect home for a magic elf.

Sending you jolly wishes and twinkling magic from the snowy realms of the North Pole!

With warm regards,

Father Christmas

P.S. Keep an eye out for Rudolph's red nose in the sky on Christmas Eve! He and the reindeer are getting ready for an unforgettable journey across the world.

Of course, if you do decide to get an elf for the class (and the time you save using AI might make this more manageable for you!), AI can write the class a letter from the elf. Furthermore, it can provide you with many ideas of things to do with the elf.

Prompt: 'Easy magic elf ideas for teachers to do with their class.'

---

1   Reading buddy: Have the elf on the shelf cosy up with a few books in the classroom library, suggesting that they love to read too.

2   Maths magician: Set up a small maths problem on the board and have the elf with a mini wand and a note saying, 'I'm here to help with magical maths!'

3   Art elf: Have the elf set up an art station with crayons, markers, and paper. Leave a note encouraging the pupils to create holiday-themed drawings.

4 Snowball fight: Arrange a mini snowball fight using cotton balls or paper balls, and place the elf with a note saying, 'Join the fun! Let's have a snowball fight!'

5 Sneaky snacker: Position the elf near a snack, like a bowl of fruit or a plate of biscuits, with a note saying, 'I couldn't resist a little treat!'

6 Helpful elf: Place the elf near supplies like pencils, rubbers, or paper and leave a note saying, 'I'm here to help you with your schoolwork!'

7 Holiday countdown: Have the elf hold a sign that counts down the days until the winter break, creating anticipation for the upcoming holidays.

8 Gift wrapper: Set up the elf with a small box and wrapping paper. Leave a note saying, 'I'm practising my gift-wrapping skills!'

9 Music lover: Place the elf near musical instruments or a CD player with a note saying, 'I love music! Let's have a dance party!'

10 Scientist elf: Arrange the elf with some simple science experiments or materials, with a note saying, 'Let's explore some holiday science together!'

11 Explorer elf: Position the elf with a magnifying glass and a note suggesting that they're on a classroom adventure, exploring different parts of the room.

12 Writing helper: Have the elf hold a pencil and paper with a note saying, 'I'm here to inspire your creative writing!'

13 Morning greeter: Place the elf near the classroom door with a sign that says, 'Good morning! Welcome to a new day of learning!'

14 Elf's favourite things: Set up a little scene with the elf's favourite toys, books, or items and leave a note saying, 'These are a few of my favourite things!'

15 Elf's thank you: Arrange the elf holding a small 'thank you' sign for the pupils, expressing gratitude for their kindness and good behaviour.

Remember, the goal is to have fun and bring a bit of holiday magic to the classroom. These ideas can spark excitement and engagement among your pupils during the holiday season.

11. Teaching Literary Techniques

Onomatopoeia is one of my favourite literary devices to teach. It lends itself nicely to themes like Guy Fawkes Night – and there is now no need to spend any time thinking up examples to use!

Prompt: 'Give me examples of onomatopoeia to describe fireworks.'

Onomatopoeia words are fantastic for describing fireworks, as they imitate the sounds these dazzling displays make. Here are some examples:

1 Boom: The deep, resonating sound of an explosion.

2 Crackle: The sharp, popping noise of sparks.

3 Whizz: The high-pitched sound as a firework streaks through the sky.

4 Bang: The sudden, loud noise of a bursting firework.

5 Fizz: The soft, sizzling sound of a sparkler.

6 Pop: The small, brief noise of a firework going off.

7 Sizzle: The sound of sparks hissing as they fly through the air.

8 Snap: The sharp, cracking sound of a firework igniting.

9 Roar: The deep, powerful sound of a firework exploding.

10 Hiss: The prolonged sound of sparks as they twirl and spin.

11 Crash: The loud sound of multiple fireworks going off simultaneously.

12 Whistle: The high, piercing noise resembling a whistle as a firework ascends.

13 Flutter: The gentle, rustling sound of a firework's falling embers.

14 Chirp: The quick, cheerful sound of a firework's quick bursts.

15 Rumble: The low, continuous sound of distant fireworks.

Using these onomatopoeic words in your descriptions can vividly convey the sensory experience of watching a fireworks display.

Of course, you can ask AI to give a general list of onomatopoeic words or experiment with other themes such as 'winter':

1 Crunch: The sound of footsteps on fresh snow.

2 Crackle: The icy sound of frozen branches or leaves.

3 Whisper: The soft, hushed sound of a gentle snowfall.

4 Swoosh: The noise of skis or sledges gliding over snow.

5 Squeak: The high-pitched sound of walking on icy surfaces.

6 Chill: The shivery feeling associated with cold weather.

7 Creak: The sound of freezing surfaces expanding and contracting.

8 Glisten: The sparkling, reflective effect of ice and snow.

9 Hush: The calm, quiet stillness that often accompanies snowfall.

10 Flutter: The light, airy sound of snowflakes falling.

11 Brrr: The exclamation people make when feeling cold.

12 Shiver: The involuntary trembling caused by cold temperatures.

13 Slush: The wet, sloshing sound of melted snow and ice.

14 Drip: The sound of icicles melting and water droplets falling.

15 Crisp: The sharp feeling of cold air and snow.

16 Frost: The delicate, crystalline formation on surfaces.

17 Tinkle: The sound of frozen objects hitting each other.

18 Patter: The rhythmic sound of freezing rain hitting surfaces.

These onomatopoeic words can help to add sensory and descriptive elements to your writing about winter scenes and experiences.

Of course, any teacher can generate a decent list of examples of onomatopoeia, but it can be time-consuming. Instead, you can now spend this time printing appealing winter-themed bordered paper for the children to write on, working on differentiated writing tasks, designing an accompanying PowerPoint or anything else to optimise the lesson.

12. Persuasive Writing

AI can save you a lot of time when planning persuasive or discursive writing by quickly generating reasons for and against an issue. For example, if you want the children to write a persuasive piece on whether school uniform should be compulsory, AI could produce a given number of reasons for or against, which they can choose from to focus on in their writing.

Prompt: 'Give me seven reasons in support of school uniform and seven reasons against school uniform.'

Reasons in support of school uniform:

1   Equality and inclusivity: School uniforms create a sense of unity among pupils regardless of their socio-economic background, reducing visible differences and promoting inclusivity.

2   Reduced peer pressure: Uniforms eliminate the pressure to wear trendy or expensive clothes, fostering a more focused and supportive learning environment.

3   Improved focus on learning: Uniforms create a clear distinction between school and leisure attire, helping pupils to mentally transition into a learning mindset.

4   Enhanced safety: Identifiable uniforms make it easier for staff to recognise intruders and ensure the safety of all pupils within the premises.

5   Professionalism and discipline: Uniforms instil a sense of discipline, responsibility, and respect for rules, preparing pupils for future workplaces.

6   Reduced bullying and judgement: Uniforms minimise opportunities for bullying related to clothing choices, allowing pupils to be valued for their personalities and talents.

7   Cost savings: Uniforms can be more cost-effective for families in the long run, as they reduce the need for a large variety of clothing options.

Reasons against school uniform:

1 Individuality and self-expression: School uniforms may restrict pupils' ability to express their individuality, creativity, and personal style.

2 Limited comfort: Uniforms might not cater to all body types, causing discomfort for some pupils who may not find them well-fitting or comfortable.

3 Restriction of freedom: Enforcing a uniform dress code can be seen as limiting pupils' freedom to choose their clothing, potentially causing resentment.

4 Lack of pupil input: Pupils may feel left out of the decision-making process regarding their attire, leading to a sense of powerlessness.

5 Uniform costs: While uniforms can be cost-effective in some cases, initial expenses can be a burden for families struggling financially.

6 Real-world transition: Some argue that uniform policies do not adequately prepare pupils for the diverse dress codes they will encounter in their future careers.

7 Focusing on appearance: Overemphasis on uniforms may shift the focus from personal growth, character development, and academic achievements.

When considering the pros and cons of school uniforms, it is important to take into account the specific context of each school and community, as well as the values and priorities of the educational institution and its stakeholders.

13. Teaching Punctuation

In addition to supporting lesson planning around the subject of punctuation, AI can provide numerous examples of usage, which can often be an onerous task.

Prompt: 'Give me example of speech marks in sentences for children to learn from.'

1 'Hello,' said Sarah to her friend.
2 'What's your favourite colour?' asked mum.
3 John exclaimed, 'Look at that beautiful rainbow!'
4 'I love ice cream,' said Tim with a grin.
5 'Can we go to the park?' begged Lily.
6 'I'm excited for the party tomorrow!' shouted Emily.
7 'Do you want to play catch?' asked Jake.
8 'The cat is on the roof!' yelled Tom.
9 'Let's build a sandcastle,' suggested Mia.
10 'I'm feeling sleepy,' yawned Alex.

In each of these sentences, the speech marks indicate the words spoken by a character. This helps readers to understand who is talking and when someone is communicating in the text. It is important for children to recognise and use speech marks accurately to enhance their writing and communication skills.

Prompt: 'Give me 10 sentences with the speech marks missing for children to identify where they should go.'

1 Tim asked Can I have a piece of cake please?
2 Mum said Dinner is ready come to the table.
3 Look at that beautiful bird exclaimed Sarah.
4 I'm going to the park said Jack.
5 What's your favourite subject in school asked Lisa.
6 The dog barked loudly Look out!

7   Can we go swimming tomorrow begged Emily.

8   It's so hot outside said Dad.

9   Let's go on an adventure suggested Alex.

10 My favourite colour is blue said Lily with a smile.

Challenge the children to insert the speech marks (and any other necessary punctuation) to make the sentences grammatically correct.

14. Character Descriptions for Literacy

Learning to create and describe characters is an important aspect of developing literacy. AI can help you to generate character descriptions from known characters and support the children to create new ones.

Prompt: 'Write a character description of Willy Wonka based on the novel *Charlie and the Chocolate Factory*.'

Willy Wonka is a captivating character from the novel *Charlie and the Chocolate Factory* by Roald Dahl. With his eccentric appearance, mysterious demeanour, and unmatched creativity, Willy Wonka stands out as a central figure in the story.

Physically, Willy Wonka is described as having a peculiar appearance that reflects his imaginative nature. He is portrayed as a small man with twinkling eyes that seem to hold endless secrets. His face is often wreathed in mischievous smiles, hinting at his playful personality. His attire is equally distinctive, with colourful and flamboyant clothing that adds to his whimsical aura.

Beyond his physical appearance, Willy Wonka's character is defined by his enigmatic and eccentric behaviour. He is the reclusive owner of the renowned Wonka Chocolate Factory, known for its fantastical creations. Wonka's enthusiasm for his work is contagious, and he exudes an air of childlike wonder despite his advanced age.

Wonka's creativity knows no bounds. He has an uncanny ability to dream up the most extraordinary and magical confections, from Three-Course Dinner Chewing Gum to Everlasting Gobstoppers. His inventiveness is matched only by his desire to delight and amaze, often pushing the boundaries of what is considered possible.

However, Wonka's eccentricity also comes with an air of mystery. He is known to be secretive and unpredictable, leaving those around him unsure of his intentions. His complex personality is a mix of brilliance, quirkiness, and a hint of underlying sadness.

Throughout the story, Willy Wonka acts as a catalyst for adventure and discovery. He invites a group of children to tour his factory, with the promise of a lifetime supply of chocolate for one lucky winner. This journey through the factory not only showcases his imaginative creations but also reveals the moral lessons he seeks to impart to the children.

In the end, Willy Wonka emerges as a multifaceted character with an undeniable impact on the narrative. His blend of creativity, mystery, and a touch of melancholy makes him a truly memorable and iconic figure in children's literature.

AI can generate excellent descriptions based on physical appearance and character with lots of interesting vocabulary for the children to master.

Prompt: 'Invent another child character for *Charlie and the Chocolate Factory*, a girl who is clever, intelligent, and polite. Write a character description.'

Amelia Everly

Amelia Everly is a brilliant addition to the cast of characters in *Charlie and the Chocolate Factory*. With her exceptional intellect, quick wit, and impeccable manners, Amelia stands out as a role model of cleverness and kindness.

Physically, Amelia is portrayed as a young girl with an air of sophistication. Her chestnut hair is often neatly tied back, allowing her sparkling blue eyes to shine. Her posture is poised and dignified, reflecting her polite and respectful nature. Amelia's choice of clothing is classic and understated, showcasing her elegance and confidence.

Amelia's intelligence is unmatched, and she possesses an insatiable curiosity for the world around her. Her mind is a treasure trove of knowledge, and she often surprises others with her ability to answer even the most complex questions. She is an avid reader and has an impressive collection of books that she eagerly shares with others.

Despite her intellectual prowess, Amelia is remarkably humble. She never flaunts her intelligence but instead uses it to help others and solve problems. Her cleverness is complemented by her sharp sense of humour, which she uses to bring joy to those around her.

One of Amelia's defining traits is her unwavering kindness. She treats everyone with respect and consideration, regardless of their background or circumstances. Her politeness is genuine and heartfelt, making her a beloved figure among both children and adults.

Amelia's presence in the story adds a layer of depth and positivity. She is an advocate for fairness and justice, and her innate sense of right and wrong guides her actions. Her determination to make the world a better place is evident in her interactions with the other children and her responses to the challenges presented in the Wonka Factory.

As the story unfolds, Amelia's character evolves from a clever and polite girl to a symbol of wisdom and compassion. She embodies the idea that intelligence is not just about knowledge but also about using one's abilities to contribute positively to the world.

In *Charlie and the Chocolate Factory*, Amelia Everly serves as a shining example of intellect, kindness, and the importance of using one's talents to make a difference. Her presence enriches the narrative and leaves a lasting impression on readers of all ages.

15. World Book Day and Banned Books Celebrations

World Book Day has always been one of my favourite school days. However, we are all striving to ensure that this celebration of reading doesn't become an additional burden for families who might be facing financial challenges. After all, World Book Day is about fostering a love for reading, not about who can showcase the most Instagram-worthy costume.

Prompt: 'Can you suggest fun and free activities for school children?'

1 Character dress-up from home: Encourage pupils to dress up as their favourite book characters using items they already have at home. This promotes creativity and reduces the need for expensive costumes.

2 Virtual author visits: Arrange virtual author visits through video calls or pre-recorded videos. Authors can read from their books, share writing tips, and answer questions from pupils.

3 Book swap: Organise a book swap where pupils bring in books they have already read and exchange them with their classmates. This promotes sharing and introduces children to new books.

4 Read-aloud sessions: Have teachers, parents, or even older pupils record videos of themselves reading passages from popular children's books. Share these videos with the pupils to encourage listening and imagination.

5 Create bookmarks: Provide materials for pupils to create their own bookmarks. They can design them with artwork inspired by their favourite books and characters.

6 Literary scavenger hunt: Create a list of book-related clues or riddles that lead pupils to different parts of the school or home. At each location, they can find a hidden quote, character name, or book title.

7 Design a new book cover: Ask pupils to choose a book they love and design a new book cover for it. This allows them to showcase their artistic skills and creativity.

8 Book-themed puzzles and crosswords: Create simple word search puzzles, crossword puzzles, or other brain-teasing activities related to famous books, authors, and characters.

9   Story chain writing: Start a story with a few sentences and have each pupil add a sentence to continue the story. This collaborative activity encourages imagination and storytelling.

10 Book review or recommendation: Invite pupils to write short book reviews or recommendations for their favourite books. Share these with the class to inspire others' reading choices.

11 Character portraits: Have pupils draw or paint portraits of their favourite book characters. Display the artwork in a virtual gallery or physical space.

12 Interactive storytelling: Begin a story and ask pupils to take turns adding sentences or paragraphs. This can be done verbally in a classroom or through a shared online document.

13 Create book trailers: Challenge pupils to create short video trailers for their favourite books using simple video editing tools or apps.

14 Literary bingo: Create bingo cards with book-related themes, such as 'Read a fairy tale' or 'Read a book with animals as characters'. Pupils can mark off squares as they complete the reading challenges.

15 Author biographies: Have pupils research and write short biographies about their favourite authors. This can be shared with the class to learn about different writers.

Remember to tailor these activities to different age groups and ensure they align with the interests of your pupils. The goal is to make World Book Day enjoyable, educational, and inclusive for all children.

There is another book-related event that I value highly, Banned Books Week, which takes place every autumn, typically during the final weekend of September. Initiated in 1982 as a response to concerns about the increasing challenges posed to books in libraries, shops, and schools, Banned Books Week is a celebration of the freedom to read.[1]

---

1   Book banning is most reported on in the USA but there have been recent media reports suggesting it becoming more of a problem in the UK. For example, Birmingham City Council's website states that Harry Potter has been banned in some UK Christian schools: https://www.birmingham.gov.uk/info/50138/leisure_and_learning/1435/censored_-_the_books_they_didnt_want_us_to_read/5. There was the recent case of the church banning a gay author who had been booked for a school visit: https://www.theguardian.com/books/2022/mar/09/catholic-church-bans-visit-by-gay-author-to-london-school. I was also recently contacted by a teacher in Glasgow who was told to remove 'unsuitable books' from her school library and I know another teacher personally who has had parents contact her head teacher and ask for books that they disapprove of to be removed from her classroom.

The event presents a wonderful opportunity for schools as it lends an air of edginess and rebellion to the act of reading. Remarkably, even books that are completely appropriate for their respective age groups – often on important subjects like the Holocaust, such as *Maus* by Art Spiegelman or *The Diary of Anne Frank* – face challenges and bans. While I concede that these books might be upsetting for young children, older pupils can be profoundly impacted by Anne Frank's story. As educators, we are constantly evaluating the suitability of the materials we introduce to our pupils, but AI can help us to carefully select excerpts that offer valuable insights.

Prompt: 'Can you give me an excerpt from Anne Frank's diary that is suitable for children to hear?'

July 15, 1944

Dear Kitty,

A bundle of contradictions. That's what I am. I have a will of iron, but at the same time, I'm as changeable as the weather. My heart is pure, and my soul is free. I'm really very understanding, but only if I feel like it. Insensitive, but also sentimental. Kind, but also mean. Trusting, but also suspicious. Lazy, and yet energetic. Funny, but also serious. I'm such a mix.

This passage captures Anne's self-reflection and the complexity of her feelings and personality. It is a glimpse into her thoughts and emotions during her time in hiding. Keep in mind that while this excerpt is suitable for children, Anne Frank's diary as a whole contains deeper and more complex content that might need further discussion with older pupils.

Prompt: 'Can you give me a list of banned children's books?'

1   *The Adventures of Huckleberry Finn* by Mark Twain: Banned for its racial themes and language, though it is also considered a classic of American literature.

2   *To Kill a Mockingbird* by Harper Lee: Banned for its discussion of racial themes, language, and mature content.

3   *Alice's Adventures in Wonderland* by Lewis Carroll: Banned in some places for its perceived nonsensical and potentially confusing content.

4 *Charlotte's Web* by E. B. White: Banned in some places due to concerns about anthropomorphism and themes of death.

5 *The Diary of Anne Frank* by Anne Frank: Banned in some places for its depictions of sensitive themes related to the Holocaust and Anne's coming of age.

6 *Where the Wild Things Are* by Maurice Sendak: Banned for its perceived dark and disturbing content, though it is celebrated for its creativity.

7 *James and the Giant Peach* by Roald Dahl: Banned in some places due to concerns about its dark and potentially frightening content.

8 *A Light in the Attic* by Shel Silverstein: Banned for its humour, irreverence, and occasionally dark themes.

9 *The Absolutely True Diary of a Part-Time Indian* by Sherman Alexie: Banned for its language, sexual content, and portrayal of challenging topics.

10 'Captain Underpants' series by Dav Pilkey: Banned for its perceived irreverence, bathroom humour, and disrespect for authority.

11 *And Tango Makes Three* by Justin Richardson and Peter Parnell: Banned for its portrayal of a same-sex penguin couple raising a chick.

12 *The Giver* by Lois Lowry: Banned for its themes of dystopia, censorship, and questioning authority.

Of course, not all these suggestions would be suitable for primary-age pupils, although I think selected parts of *The Diary of Anne Frank* certainly could be. I already have my own favourite banned books, including *And Tango Makes Three*, which is a lovely and age-appropriate book for lower primary.

16. Grammar and Punctuation Examples

When it comes to teaching features of language, it is useful to be able to show children lots of examples. For instance, Key Stage 2/Second Level writing includes pupils being able to use 'moreover' as a connective. AI can give you lots of illustrations of this.

Prompt: 'Give me four child-friendly sentences with "moreover" used as a connective.'

---

1   I love playing football; moreover, I enjoy riding my bike with friends.

2   My favourite colour is blue; moreover, I like drawing pictures of the sky and ocean.

3   I have a pet cat; moreover, I dream of having a dog someday.

4   I enjoy reading adventure stories; moreover, I like solving puzzles in my free time.

We can employ the same technique with punctuation – for example, 'Give me four child-friendly sentences with speech marks included.'

---

1   The teacher said, 'Class, it's time for our art project.'

2   Sarah exclaimed, 'Look at the rainbow in the sky!'

3   My dad asked, 'Would you like some ice cream for dessert?'

4   Tom whispered to his friend, 'Let's explore the mysterious cave together.'

Or 'What are the rules for using a semicolon in a sentence?' (I must admit that this is the one piece of punctuation that throws me.)

Semicolons are used to join two independent clauses (complete thoughts) that are closely related and could stand alone as separate sentences. Here are the rules for using a semicolon in writing:

1   Connecting independent clauses: Use a semicolon to connect two independent clauses that are related in content. Do not use a conjunction (like 'and', 'but', 'or') before the semicolon.

    Example: 'I enjoy painting; it helps me to relax.'

---

2   Separating items in a list: When you have a list of items that already contain commas, you can use semicolons to separate the items.

Example: 'She bought apples, bananas, and oranges; a watermelon; and a bunch of grapes.'

3   Joining independent clauses with transitional phrases: If you use a transitional phrase (such as 'however', 'therefore', 'for example') to connect two independent clauses, you can use a semicolon before the transitional phrase.

Example: 'The weather was bad; however, we still managed to have a great time.'

Remember that semicolons should be used sparingly and appropriately. They are meant to provide clarity and enhance the flow of your writing. It is essential to understand the relationship between the clauses you are connecting and to avoid using semicolons where a period or a conjunction might be more appropriate.

17. Teaching Genres

I enjoy teaching literary genres, but finding multiple examples of each genre can be time-consuming, especially if you end up having to produce your own. AI can generate short stories in a range of genres, which makes creating an assessment on this topic an effortless process.

Prompt: 'Create a genres assessment where children need to read short passages and identify the genre of each passage (provide the answers at the end).'

Genres Assessment: Identify the Genre

Read each passage below and identify the genre of each passage. Choose from the following options: fiction, non-fiction, mystery, fantasy, science fiction, historical fiction, adventure, poetry.

Passage 1:

The moonlit night was still as the brave knight, Sir William, ventured into the mouth of the forbidding cave. His sword gleamed in the dim light, held firmly in his gloved hand. The cavern was shrouded in an eerie silence, broken only by the distant echoes of dripping water. Sir William's heart raced as he pressed forward, driven by the urgency of his quest. His mission was clear: rescue the kidnapped princess, taken by the fearsome dragon that had terrorised the kingdom for months. As he delved deeper into the cave's depths, his mind was consumed by thoughts of the perilous battle that lay ahead.

Passage 2:

In this informative book, the author presents a comprehensive exploration of the life cycle of butterflies. With vivid illustrations that capture the delicate beauty of these insects, the reader is guided through each stage of the transformation process. From the moment a butterfly lays its eggs to the emergence of caterpillars and their eventual metamorphosis into fully grown butterflies, the book offers an engaging blend of factual information and captivating imagery. Young readers will gain a deeper understanding of the natural world and the wonder of metamorphosis.

Passage 3:

The old mansion stood atop the hill, its weathered walls cloaked in shadows. Whispers of the past seemed to echo through its halls, telling tales of bygone days and long-forgotten secrets. A group of daring friends had gathered there on a moonlit night, determined to unravel the mysteries that surrounded the haunted place. Armed with flashlights and their courage, they tiptoed through the dimly lit corridors, their hearts pounding with a mix of fear and excitement. The faintest sounds of footsteps and eerie whispers only fuelled their curiosity further. What they uncovered that night would change their lives forever.

Passage 4:

In the enchanting land of Eldoria, where magic was as real as the air they breathed, lived a young girl named Aurora. She discovered her extraordinary abilities one fateful day when a rainbow-hued phoenix landed on her windowsill, its feathers shimmering with every colour imaginable. The magical creature bestowed upon her the power to control the elements – fire, water, air, and earth. With her newfound abilities, Aurora embarked on a grand quest to save her kingdom from the clutches of an evil sorcerer who sought to plunge Eldoria into eternal darkness. Armed with her bravery and the guidance of the phoenix, Aurora's journey was filled with danger, friendship, and the unfaltering belief in the magic within.

Passage 5:

Against the sweeping canvas of the Second World War, a band of youthful comrades find themselves entwined in the intricate tapestry of life on the home front. In the shadow of distant battlefields, where their elder kin and neighbours embark upon perilous odysseys, these children remain anchored to their homeland, shouldering the burden of uncertainty and trepidation. In a world defined by rationed resources, the haunting refrain of air-raid sirens, and the relentless drumbeat of wartime propaganda, their tales began to weave.

Passage 6:

The Starship *Galactic Voyager* soared through the vast expanse of the universe, its sleek hull reflecting the myriad stars that peppered the cosmic canvas. On board, a crew of intrepid explorers embarked on a mission to discover new planets and encounter alien species. With cutting-edge technology at their disposal, they navigated through warp gates, encountering breathtaking and challenging cosmic phenomena. Their voyage was a testament to the boundless curiosity of humanity and the uncharted wonders that awaited them among the stars.

Passage 7:

> As the sun sank low, its amber light aglow,
>
> O'er meadow hushed, in tranquil grace it'd show.
>
> The flowers danced, in zephyr's tender plea,
>
> Their hues a vibrant, vivid tapestry.
>
> A symphony, the birds in chorus sing,
>
> Their evening serenade, on silent wing.
>
> A peace descends, o'er this twilight's grace,
>
> A testament to evening's gentle embrace.

Answers:

1 Adventure

2 Non-fiction

3 Mystery

4 Fantasy

5 Historical fiction

6 Science fiction

7 Poetry

You can easily make these passages longer, shorter, or more advanced to meet the needs of each child or reading group, speeding up the process of creating assessments in this area of the curriculum.

18. Generating Alternative Story Endings

AI can be utilised to create alternative story endings, which can be beneficial in teaching pupils the art of story writing. It is especially useful when children struggle to conclude a story (and resort to the cliché, 'and then I woke up and it was all a dream'!). While pupils often begin with brilliant ideas, anticipating an ending can be challenging. AI can help them to experiment with various ideas until they discover a suitable solution.

Take this AI-generated short story, for example:

In a hidden glade within a mystical forest lived Elara, a kind-hearted witch. Her cabin, made of twisted trees and adorned with herbs, stood as a sanctuary of enchantment. Elara spent her days nurturing her magical garden and fostering harmony among the woodland creatures.

One day, she discovered a mischievous pixie named Pippin caught in her curtains. They became fast friends, sharing laughter, stories, and the secrets of their worlds. Their bond grew, marked by shared adventures and enchanting spells.

As time passed, Pippin prepared to return to his realm. He gifted Elara a vial of sparkling pixie dust, a reminder of their magical connection. With a bittersweet farewell, Pippin took flight, leaving behind a tapestry of friendship and wonder.

Elara's cabin remained a beacon of enchantment, and the forest flourished under her care. Whenever she needed a touch of magic, she would release a pinch of pixie dust, and the wind would carry its whimsy through the trees.
In the heart of the woods, Elara's cabin stood as a testament to the enduring power of friendship and magic.

I can copy this story into an AI app or website and say, 'Generate an alternative ending to the following.'

In a hidden glade within a mystical forest lived Elara, a kind-hearted witch. Her cabin, made of twisted trees and adorned with herbs, stood as a sanctuary of enchantment. Elara spent her days nurturing her magical garden and fostering harmony among the woodland creatures.

One day, she discovered a mischievous pixie named Pippin caught in her curtains. They became fast friends, sharing laughter, stories, and the secrets of their worlds. Their bond grew, marked by shared adventures and enchanting spells.

As time passed, Pippin prepared to return to his realm. He gifted Elara a vial of sparkling pixie dust, a reminder of their magical connection. But instead of a farewell, Pippin shared an idea – to create a portal that would allow them to visit each other's worlds whenever they wished. With determination and a touch of magic, they wove the threads of their friendship into a spell that would bridge the gap between their realms.

The first time Elara stepped through the portal into the pixie realm, she was greeted with a breathtaking landscape of iridescent flowers and shimmering streams. Pippin introduced her to his pixie friends, and they embraced her as one of their own. Similarly, Pippin marvelled at the wonders of Elara's forest, where the trees whispered ancient secrets and the creatures spoke in riddles.

As seasons changed, Elara split her time between her forest sanctuary and the pixie realm, and Pippin visited her cabin with the same sense of wonder he felt every time he fluttered through the portal. Their worlds blended, and the barrier between witch and pixie began to dissolve.

With their powerful friendship, Elara and Pippin discovered that their combined magic had the ability to heal parts of the forest that were struggling. They worked together to mend the wounded parts of the land and bring prosperity to both realms.

Elara's cabin remained a beacon of enchantment, and the forest flourished under their shared care. The portal between their worlds became a symbol of unity and cooperation, reminding everyone that even the most different beings could find common ground and create something beautiful together. In the heart of the woods, Elara and Pippin's legacy stood as a testament to the enduring power of friendship, unity, and the magic that exists when worlds collide.

Pupils can continue typing 'and another alternative ending' until they find something they like.

19. Story Starters

You can ask AI to devise a story starter for the children to continue. Like coming up with satisfactory endings, getting started can also be a barrier to writing. Many children can write well once they have managed to get going.

Prompt: 'Write a child-friendly story starter about a magical castle'.

In a land of endless wonders and enchanted forests, there stood a magical castle that seemed to shimmer in every colour of the rainbow. Its turrets reached high into the sky, touching the clouds as if inviting curious adventurers to explore its secrets. But what made this castle truly special was its ability to grant the wishes of anyone who could solve its riddles. One sunny morning, a brave group of friends decided to embark on a journey to the castle, eager to unlock its mysteries and have their deepest desires fulfilled. As they approached the castle gates, they couldn't help but feel a sense of excitement and anticipation, wondering what challenges and enchantments awaited them within its walls …

The beauty of AI-generated story starters is that if the story starter doesn't resonate with the pupil, another can be quickly created. If you have access to an iPad or tablet, the pupil could create several story starters themselves and choose their favourite one to work with.

Prompt: 'Write a child-friendly story starter about a haunted house'.

In a quiet village, there stood a spooky old house. It was said to be haunted, with strange lights and eerie voices inside. One sunny morning, three curious children named Lily, Max, and Ben decided to investigate. Armed with flashlights and a sense of adventure, they approached the creaky path leading to the haunted house, hearts racing with excitement. What secrets would they uncover?

20. Fact Sheets and Information Resources

We are all aware of how effective fact sheets can be, especially for children with a strong interest in certain topics and a thirst for more knowledge. Fact sheets serve as an excellent introduction for young learners, teaching them how to identify relevant and intriguing information for crafting reports or catering to their unique interests.

Prompt: 'Give me 10 facts for children about the T-Rex.'

1   Mighty hunter: The T-Rex, short for *Tyrannosaurus rex*, was one of the biggest meat-eating dinosaurs that ever lived. It was a fearsome predator and hunted other dinosaurs for food.

2   Tiny arms: Despite its huge size, T-Rex had small, almost comically short arms. Scientists are still figuring out why these arms were so small, but they might have been used for balance or grabbing onto prey.

3   Sharp teeth: T-Rex had a mouth full of sharp, serrated teeth that could easily crush bone. Its bite was one of the strongest bites in the animal kingdom!

4   Big teeth, little brain: T-Rex had a large head with a brain that was relatively small compared to its body size. But that didn't stop it from being a top predator!

5   Fast: Despite its big body, T-Rex was surprisingly fast. It could run at speeds of around 20–25 miles (32–40km) per hour.

6   Fossil discoveries: The first T-Rex fossil was discovered in 1902 in Montana, USA. Since then, many more fossils have been found, helping scientists to learn more about these incredible creatures.

7   Big and heavy: Adult T-Rexes could weigh up to 9 tonnes, which is about the weight of two elephants!

8   Feathered relatives: Recent discoveries suggest that some T-Rex relatives had feathers. These feathers might have been for insulation or display rather than flight.

9   Short lifespan: T-Rex didn't live very long. Scientists estimate that they only lived to be around 28 years old, which is relatively young for such a large dinosaur.

10 Roaring sound: While no one knows exactly what T-Rex sounded like, scientists believe it might have made deep, booming roars, like a mix between a lion's roar and an elephant's trumpet.

Remember, dinosaurs like T-Rex lived a long time ago, and scientists are still learning new things about them by studying fossils and using their imaginations to piece together the past.

The fact that such resources can be so easily personalised to meet pupil or class interests helps to make the learning more engaging, which, as we all know, is at least half the battle.

21. Creating Daily VCOP Challenges

Vocabulary, connectives, openers and punctuation (VCOP) require regular thought and practice. It can be useful to have daily challenges displayed on your board for fast finishers or children who need to be stretched.

I asked AI to give me a VCOP challenge. Initially, it generated a vocabulary one, so I gave a more specific prompt: 'Can you give me three questions for vocabulary, three for connectives, three for openers and three for punctuation.'

Vocabulary:

1   Can you find a synonym for the word 'happy' that would make your story more interesting?

2   What descriptive word could you use to make the character's appearance more vivid?

3   Choose a word from your story and explain its meaning in your own words.

Connectives:

1   How can you use the word 'however' to show a contrast in your story?

2   Can you think of a connective that would help your reader understand the sequence of events better?

3   Try using the word 'because' to explain the reason behind your character's actions.

Openers:

1   Begin your story with an -ing opener to create a sense of action.

2   Start a sentence with an adverb opener to show how a character is feeling.

3   Write a sentence using a prepositional opener to describe the setting of your story.

Punctuation:

1   Where should you place a question mark in a sentence that asks for information?

2   How can you use a comma to separate items in a list?

3   Rewrite a sentence using an exclamation mark to show excitement or surprise.

---

22. Teaching Children Who Are Learning English

Over the years, I have had the pleasure of teaching many 'New Scots', most of whom were children who had arrived in Scotland as refugees. It was an honour to assist these children in settling in, learning aspects of their native language, helping them to grasp English, and building connections with them. As you might expect, translators are often in short supply, which is where AI can prove indispensable!

Consider a scenario where you are engaging in a winter-themed topic (perhaps even with the luxury of some snow). You could request AI to devise some simple instructions for constructing an igloo – instructions that can subsequently be translated into any language.

How to build an igloo

Materials:

- Packed snow
- Shovel
- Snow blocks (pre-cut or made using a mould)
- Cold weather clothing and gloves
- Patience and a sense of adventure!

Step-by-step instructions:

1 Choose a suitable location: Find a flat area with enough snow that has been packed by the wind or has settled for a while. Avoid areas with uneven terrain or potential avalanche risks.

2 Mark the base: Use your shovel to clear an area and mark the shape of your igloo's base. A circular or slightly oval shape works well. Make it around 2–3 metres in diameter.

3 Create the entrance: Decide where you want the entrance to be. This will be a smaller, tunnel-like entrance to help retain heat inside the igloo. Dig a trench about 60–90 cm wide and a couple of feet long, sloping downward from the base to the outside.

4 Start making snow blocks: Use a shovel to cut out rectangular snow blocks from the surrounding area. The blocks should be around 60 cm

long, 30 cm wide, and about 15–20 cm thick. You can also make a mould to create consistent blocks.

5 Begin building the walls: Place the first snow block at the base of your marked circle. Press it firmly into the snow to ensure stability. Continue adding blocks around the base in a circular pattern, slightly angling them inward as you go. This will create a gentle curve as the walls rise.

6 Stagger the blocks: As you stack the blocks, make sure to stagger them like bricks in a wall. This helps to increase stability and prevent the igloo from collapsing.

7 Build upwards: Continue stacking the snow blocks, gradually reducing the size of the blocks as you move upward. This will help to create the classic dome shape of an igloo.

8 Create the dome: As the walls rise, you will need to gradually start angling the blocks more steeply towards the centre to create the dome shape. Make sure to leave a gap at the top where the final capstone will fit.

9 Place the capstone: Once you have built the dome, carefully cut a larger block to serve as the capstone. Gently place it on top of the dome, filling any gaps around the edges to seal the igloo.

10 Shape the interior: Use your hands or a small shovel to smooth out the interior walls. This will help to create a more comfortable and spacious interior.

11 Create a raised sleeping platform: Dig a shallow trench inside the igloo, away from the entrance. This will create a raised platform where you can lay down your sleeping bags or mats.

12 Final touches: Smooth out the entrance tunnel and build a small wall of snow blocks at the entrance to help block out cold winds.

Remember, building an igloo can take some time and effort, so be patient and work safely. It is also a good idea to have a friend with you to help and enjoy the experience together.

Here is the part I find simply amazing – you can ask AI to translate the above text into Arabic, or Chinese, or whatever language you like!

As teachers, it is our job to help children acquire a solid foundation in the English language, but anyone would agree that being able to translate text in seconds is incredibly useful. AI can help to bridge the learning gap for non-native pupils by enabling them to continue developing their mathematical understanding, critical thinking skills, and so on in their first language alongside learning English.

23. What A Good One Looks Like

As a teacher who has delved into the realm of making learning visible, I wholeheartedly endorse the What A Good One Looks Like (WAGOLL) approach. Nevertheless, sourcing or crafting suitable writing examples week after week can take up a substantial amount of time. Whether the children are immersed in creative writing, report writing, or any other genre, the pursuit of finding suitable samples often leads me down a path of editing existing pieces or generating entirely new ones. AI offers a speedy solution to the creation of well-crafted WAGOLLs that encapsulate the precise elements you intend to teach. Let's look at an example of what AI can do.

Prompt: 'Write an example of a good persuasive letter (for 10-year-olds) to a politician, arguing for fireworks to be banned. Include a range of persuasive sentence openers.'

Dear [Politician's Name],

I hope this letter finds you in good health and high spirits. My name is [Your Name], and I am a 10-year-old pupil from [Your Constituency]. I am writing to you today to express my concerns about the use of fireworks and to kindly request your support in banning them.

First and foremost, fireworks can be extremely dangerous. Every year, countless accidents occur due to the mishandling or misuse of fireworks. These accidents can cause severe injuries, burns, and even fires. As children, we should be able to enjoy celebrations without worrying about our safety. By banning fireworks, we can prevent these accidents and ensure a safer environment for everyone.

Moreover, fireworks can be harmful to the environment. The loud noises and bright lights can disturb wildlife, especially birds and other animals. They can cause stress, disorientation, and even harm to their delicate hearing. Additionally, the chemicals used in fireworks can pollute the air and water, harming our environment and the creatures that depend upon it. By banning fireworks, we can protect our environment and show our commitment to being responsible stewards of the Earth.

Furthermore, fireworks can be distressing for people with sensory sensitivities or those who suffer from anxiety or post-traumatic stress disorder. The loud noises and sudden bursts of light can trigger panic attacks and create a sense of fear and discomfort. As a compassionate society, it is our duty to ensure that everyone can enjoy celebrations without feeling anxious or scared. Banning fireworks would be a step towards inclusivity and empathy for those who struggle with sensory issues.

In addition to the safety and environmental concerns, banning fireworks would also save a significant amount of money. Fireworks displays require a substantial budget, which could be better utilised for other important purposes. For instance, the funds could be allocated towards improving schools, parks, or healthcare facilities. By redirecting these resources, we can invest in the well-being and education of our community, benefitting everyone in the long run.

In conclusion, I strongly believe that banning fireworks is a necessary step towards creating a safer, more inclusive, and environmentally friendly society. By doing so, we can prevent accidents, protect wildlife, support individuals with sensory sensitivities, and allocate resources more effectively. I kindly request your support in considering this matter and taking action to ban fireworks.

Thank you for your time and attention. I hope you will consider the concerns raised in this letter and take the necessary steps to make our community a better place for all.

Yours sincerely,

[Your Name]

If the example generated isn't exactly what you want, you can ask the app to 'shorten the above' and so on. Easy!

24. Self-Assessment of Writing

'Two stars and a wish' is a popular form of assessment for children's writing, but it can be quite time-consuming to implement. Unbelievably, AI can do this for you! If the children have been typing stories, for example, they can copy and paste them into an AI app and request a 'two stars and a wish' evaluation. They might even guide the AI to provide more specific feedback, such as 'Give two stars and a wish focusing on punctuation usage.'

This approach empowers children to self-assess and take ownership of their learning. They can seek immediate feedback, incorporate the improvements suggested in the wish, and then make the necessary changes before finalising their work. While children appreciate receiving feedback from their teacher, if used strategically – perhaps on alternate pieces of writing – this method can significantly cut down on marking time.

25. Teaching Modern Languages

When I was in high school, German was considered an exceedingly useful language to learn, especially for business. I had a strong affection for the German language and became quite proficient. During my teacher training, I eagerly anticipated the opportunity to instruct a class in German. I also enjoyed how similar German sounded to my native Glasgow accent, which greatly facilitated my pronunciation.

However, the school where I was placed during my NQT year required French and Spanish for the modern languages curriculum. Undeterred, I managed to navigate this challenge, hoping I would get an opportunity to teach German the following year. Sadly, it was not to be. Once again, I secured a position at a school where the focus was on French and Spanish.

The crux of my observation is this: as primary teachers, we are not always expert in the languages our schools decide to prioritise (and, in all fairness, schools are justified in insisting on which languages they want taught to ensure consistency for the children). However, AI can ease the process of teaching languages, especially those with which we are less familiar.

For example, entering 'Plan a children's French lesson on food and provide English pronunciation' produces the following:

Exploring French Food: Bon Appétit!

Objective: To introduce children to basic French food vocabulary and cultural aspects related to food, fostering an appreciation for French cuisine.

Materials:

- Pictures or flashcards of various French foods
- Paper and colouring materials
- Optional: French music or recordings of French food-related phrases

Lesson plan:

1   Introduction (5 minutes):

- Begin by asking the children if they have tried any French foods or if they know any French words related to food.
- Explain that France is famous for its delicious cuisine and that we will be learning some French food words today.

2   Basic food vocabulary (10 minutes):

- Introduce basic French food vocabulary, using pictures or flashcards to aid understanding.
- Teach the following words and their English pronunciation:
  - Bread (*pain*) – pronounced 'pan'
  - Cheese (*fromage*) – pronounced 'froh-mahzh'
  - Croissant – pronounced 'kwa-sahn'
  - Chocolate (*chocolat*) – pronounced 'sho-ko-la'
  - Apple (*pomme*) – pronounced 'pohm'
  - Ice cream (*glace*) – pronounced 'glahs'
  - Pizza – pronounced 'pee-tsa'
  - Pancake (*crêpe*) – pronounced 'krep'
  - Carrot (*carotte*) – pronounced 'ka-rott'
  - Tomato (*tomate*) – pronounced 'toh-maht'

3   Cultural aspects (10 minutes):

- Discuss the importance of food in French culture, such as the tradition of enjoying long meals with family and friends.
- Mention famous French dishes like croissants, baguettes, and crêpes, and explain their significance in French cuisine.
- Optional: Play French music or recordings of French food-related phrases to create a lively atmosphere.

4   Colouring French foods activity (15 minutes):

- Distribute paper and colouring materials to the children.
- Provide them with colouring sheets featuring various French foods.
- Encourage them to colour the foods while practicing the French words and their English pronunciation.

5   Food tasting (15 minutes):

- Prepare a small selection of French foods for the children to taste, such as a baguette, some cheese, or a croissant.
- Explain the importance of trying new foods and experiencing different flavours.

- Allow the children to taste the foods and encourage them to describe the flavours and textures.

6 Conclusion (5 minutes):

- Recap the main French food vocabulary learned during the lesson.
- Ask the children if they enjoyed the food tasting and if they have any questions or comments about French cuisine.
- Emphasise the importance of exploring different cultures and their culinary traditions.

Note: It is important to consider any dietary restrictions or allergies the children may have when planning the food tasting portion. Additionally, adapt the lesson plan to the age group and language proficiency level of the children, ensuring it is presented in an engaging and age-appropriate manner.

Oh, and just to complete this section, I never did get to teach German! *Macht nichts!*

26. Enhancing Language with AI Translation

AI-assisted translation is an exciting way to enrich children's writing and language skills. The pupils could compose a simple short story or passage and then request AI to translate it into a language they are currently learning. Subsequently, they could attempt to read the translated story, discern what they can pronounce accurately, identify familiar words, and learn new vocabulary or phrases. This process is an engaging and interactive way for children to strengthen both their language skills and storytelling abilities.

For example, a child might write a story about a cat:

Poor Whiskers?

Once there was a furry cat called Whiskers. Whiskers was a very curious cat.

One beautiful sunny day, Whiskers looked out of the window. He saw birds flying high in the sky. 'I want to fly like the birds,' thought Whiskers. So, he tried to jump really high, but he couldn't fly like the birds.

Next, Whiskers saw a squirrel climbing a tall tree. 'I want to climb like the squirrel,' thought Whiskers. So, he scampered up the tree, but he couldn't climb like the squirrel.

Whiskers was so sad but then he realised he can purr, cuddle, and be the best cat in the world!

Prompt: 'Translate the following into Spanish.'

¿Pobre Whiskers?

Había una vez un gato peludo llamado Whiskers. Whiskers era un gato muy curioso.

Un hermoso día soleado, Whiskers miró por la ventana. Vio pájaros volando alto en el cielo. 'Quiero volar como los pájaros,' pensó Whiskers. Así que intentó saltar muy alto, pero no pudo volar como los pájaros.

Después, Whiskers vio una ardilla trepando un árbol alto. 'Quiero trepar como la ardilla,' pensó Whiskers. Entonces, subió corriendo por el árbol, pero no pudo trepar como la ardilla.

Whiskers estaba muy triste, pero luego se dio cuenta de que puede ronronear, acurrucarse y ser el mejor gato del mundo!

27. Translating Names Across Languages

When learning about a country that uses a different alphabet, children enjoy seeing what their name would look like in that language. Depending on the focus of the lesson, this can also lend itself to a nice calligraphy activity. Furthermore, this exercise can foster empathy by enabling pupils to see how challenging it can be to learn a second language that uses different graphemes.

First, you could prompt: 'Give me six random girls' names and six random boys' names.'

Girls' names:
1 Olivia
2 Mia
3 Ava
4 Lily
5 Sophia
6 Emma

Boys' names:
1 Liam
2 Noah
3 Ethan
4 Jackson
5 Oliver
6 Lucas

The names could be translated into the mother tongue of their fellow classmates – for example, girls' names in Chinese:

1 Olivia – 奥利维亚 (Àolìwéiyà)
2 Mia – 米娅 (Mǐyà)
3 Ava – 阿娃 (Āwá)
4 Lily – 莉莉 (Lìlì)

5   Sophia – 索菲亚 (Suǒfēiyà)

6   Emma – 艾玛 (Àimǎ)

Or boys' names in Punjabi:

1   Liam – ਲਿਅਮ

2   Noah – ਨੋਆਹ

3   Ethan – ਈਥਨ

4   Jackson – ਜੈਕਸਨ

5   Oliver – ਆਲੀਵਰ

6   Lucas – ਲੂਕਸ

Please note that these transliterations are based on the pronunciation of the names in Punjabi and may not necessarily be the exact phonetic representation.

28. Maths Drills

While teachers understand the significance of incorporating a creative element to make maths engaging and meaningful, the task of generating questions for pupils to tackle can be onerous. This is especially true with older classes, where crafting questions and answers can be particularly demanding. Just as with spelling, AI can simplify the process of differentiation and reduce the time spent on creating maths questions. I have found it to be especially effective in generating extension activities for advanced pupils who require additional challenge to remain engaged and intellectually stimulated.

For example, inputting 'Give me five maths questions, multiplying 3 digit numbers by 1 digit with answers' into an AI app generates:

1   Question: Multiply 345 by 7.

    Answer: 2,415

2   Question: Multiply 512 by 4.

    Answer: 2,048

3   Question: Multiply 876 by 9.

    Answer: 7,884

4   Question: Multiply 789 by 3.

    Answer: 2,367

5   Question: Multiply 987 by 6.

    Answer: 5,922

The key is to be exact about the questions that are required (we are usually focusing on specific maths operations and patterns anyway).

For example, you can ask for 4-digit numbers multiplied by 6, or division questions, or use AI to plan for extra challenge: 'Give me three similar questions but worded problems (with answers).'

1 Question: Sarah bought 5 packs of pencils, with each pack containing 345 pencils. How many pencils did Sarah buy in total?

Answer: Sarah bought a total of 1,725 pencils. (345 x 5 = 1,725)

2 Question: A farmer has 8 fields, and each field has 789 apple trees. How many apple trees are there in total?

Answer: There are a total of 6,312 apple trees. (789 x 8 = 6,312)

3 Question: A bakery sells 3 cakes, with each cake weighing 876 grams. What is the total weight of the cakes sold?

Answer: The total weight of the cakes sold is 2,628 grams. (876 x 3 = 2,628)

With differentiation so quick and easy, it is possible to shape the curriculum to the children's interests, making the learning more engaging. You can use AI to make worded maths problems to fit with a particular theme or subject the children enjoy – for example, 'Give me a divide by 7 maths problem involving Minions' gives:

There are 7 Minions in a banana factory. If the 343 bananas are to be equally distributed among all the Minions, how many bananas will each Minion receive?

There is endless potential for using AI in maths lessons – for money problems, capacity and volume, or times tables practice. It can also be used for self-assessment purposes, which teaches pupils about the need to input numbers accurately. If they haven't got the correct answer, have they made a mistake in the calculation or have they made an error inputting the numbers? AI is a form of technology that the children need to learn how to use correctly (much like when they learn that if they type 'two' instead of 'too', a spell-checker might not recognise it as an error).

29. Maths, Baking, and Real-Life Contexts

Primary teachers know that baking serves as an excellent way to contextualise mathematics and introduce measurements in a captivating and enjoyable way. However, we also understand that the challenge lies not in the enjoyable process of measuring and mixing, but rather in transforming the ingredients into a palatable snack! This issue often arises if we have limited facilities or there are concerns about the risks associated with exposing children to a hot oven – a dilemma amplified in today's culture of blame.

AI offers a solution by providing a repository of 'no-bake' recipes, enabling children to engage in the exciting process of measuring and mixing – the moments brimming with enjoyment and learning – and savour the end result.

When I typed in 'No-bake cookies for children,' the first recipe gave me measurements in cups, so I simply typed in, 'Give me the above with ingredients in grammes.'

No-Bake Chocolate Banana Oat Cookies

Ingredients:

- 2 ripe bananas, mashed
- 150 g rolled oats
- 25 g cocoa powder
- 60 g honey or maple syrup
- 60 ml milk (dairy or plant-based)
- 2.5 ml vanilla extract
- Pinch of salt
- Optional add-ins: mini chocolate chips, chopped nuts, dried fruit

Instructions:

1. In a mixing bowl, combine the mashed bananas, rolled oats, and cocoa powder.

2. Add honey (or maple syrup), milk, vanilla extract, and a pinch of salt. Mix well until all the ingredients are thoroughly combined.

3. If desired, add optional add-ins like mini chocolate chips, chopped nuts, or dried fruit. Mix to distribute evenly.

4 Use a spoon or your hands to scoop portions of the mixture and shape them into cookies. Place them on a parchment-paper-lined tray.

5 Let the cookies set in the refrigerator for about 1–2 hours, or until they firm up.

6 Once the cookies have set, they are ready to enjoy!

Enjoy making these no-bake chocolate banana oat cookies with the kids and have a delightful and educational time in the kitchen!

I have also made some AI-generated soup recipes, which have yielded lovely results, effectively streamlining both my lunch preparations and my lesson planning!

30. Mathematical Ideas

Some parts of the primary maths curriculum are based on conceptual ideas, such as probability, and often there aren't many practice questions available to download. AI can plan and resource these lessons for you.

For example, you can ask: 'Can you plan me a lesson to introduce children to the mathematical concept of probability?'

Introduction to Probability

Stage: Key Stage 2

Objective: By the end of the lesson, pupils will be able to understand and use basic probability terms and calculate simple probabilities.

Materials:

- Coin
- Six-sided die
- Deck of playing cards
- A whiteboard or chart paper
- Markers
- Probability worksheets (optional)

Lesson duration: 45–60 minutes

Lesson steps:

1 Introduction (10 minutes):
  - Start the lesson by discussing what probability means. Explain that probability is the likelihood of something happening.
  - Use relatable examples: 'What is the probability of it raining today? What is the probability of flipping heads on a coin?'

2 Vocabulary (10 minutes):
  - Introduce key probability terms:
    - Outcome: A possible result of an event.
    - Event: A specific set of outcomes.

- Certain: Probability of 1 (100% chance).
- Impossible: Probability of 0 (0% chance).
- Likely: Probability between 0.5 and 1.
- Unlikely: Probability between 0 and 0.5.

3 Coin toss activity (10 minutes):

- Have a volunteer toss a coin, and ask the class to predict the outcome (heads or tails). Record their predictions on the board.
- Toss the coin and record the actual outcome.
- Discuss the results and calculate the probability of getting heads or tails.

4 Die-rolling activity (10 minutes):

- Have a volunteer roll a six-sided die, and ask the class to predict the outcome (1, 2, 3, 4, 5, or 6). Record their predictions.
- Roll the die and record the actual outcome.
- Calculate the probability of each outcome and discuss.

5 Card-drawing activity (10 minutes):

- Use a deck of playing cards and explain that there are 52 cards in a standard deck.
- Ask a pupil to draw a card (without looking) and predict whether it will be red (hearts or diamonds) or black (clubs or spades). Record their predictions.
- Have the pupil draw a card and record the actual outcome.
- Calculate the probability of drawing a red or black card.

6 Conclusion (5 minutes):

- Summarise the key concepts learned during the lesson.
- Provide pupils with probability worksheets for additional practice (optional).
- Encourage questions and a discussion about real-life situations where probability can be applied.

Homework (optional):

- Provide pupils with probability-related questions or scenarios to solve at home. This reinforces their understanding of the concept.

Assessment:

- Assess pupils' understanding through participation, their ability to predict and calculate probabilities, and their responses to homework assignments (if given).

You can then ask AI to provide some written practice questions for the next lesson:

Basic probability:

1 What is the probability of rolling a 4 on a standard six-sided die?

2 If you have a bag with four red marbles and six blue marbles, what is the probability of picking a red marble randomly?

3 If you toss a fair coin, what is the probability of getting tails?

4 In a deck of cards, what is the probability of drawing a face card (king, queen, or jack)?

5 If you have a spinner divided into four equal sections (A, B, C, and D), what is the probability of it landing on section C?

More challenging probability:

6 If you roll two dice, what is the probability of getting a sum of 7?

7 In a jar, there are 12 marbles: five red, three blue, and four green. What is the probability of picking a red or blue marble at random?

8 You have a bag with eight marbles: three are yellow, two are green, and three are red. What is the probability of picking a yellow marble followed by a red marble (without replacement)?

9 In a deck of cards, what is the probability of drawing a red card followed by a black card (without replacement)?

10 If you spin a spinner divided into six equal sections, what is the probability of it landing on a multiple of 3 (3 or 6)?

Feel free to adapt these questions to the level and needs of your pupils. You can also create additional questions or scenarios to further challenge their understanding of probability.

Using AI for maths not only speeds up lesson planning but also ensures breadth and depth. It is possible to generate contextualised assessments in a similar way. This can free up time to undertake other tasks, such as displaying pupil work, creating display walls, and so on.

31. Teaching Money

As teachers, we understand the importance of framing maths concepts to show their relevance in real life. When teaching children about money, it is easy to produce a menu for an appealing restaurant along with some accompanying questions. These can even be presented in a 'chilli challenge' form.

Prompt: 'Create a menu for a Japanese restaurant to appeal to children with prices next to the food (in British pounds).'

Kid's Menu – Kawaii Japanese Delights

- Mini Ramen Bowl – delicious, slurp-worthy ramen noodles with a mild broth – £5.99
- Teriyaki Chicken Bites – tender chicken pieces glazed with sweet teriyaki sauce – £6.49
- Crispy Tempura Shrimp – crunchy tempura shrimp served with a tangy dipping sauce – £7.99
- Cute Sushi Rolls – mini sushi rolls with cucumber, avocado, and crab – £8.49
- Yummy Bento Box – a mix of chicken yakitori, steamed rice, and edamame – £9.99
- Mini Okonomiyaki Pancake – savoury Japanese pancake with veggies and your choice of topping – £7.49
- Sweet Mochi Ice Cream – soft mochi rice cakes with a scoop of ice cream (vanilla or matcha) – £4.99

Side orders

- Edamame Pods – steamed young soybean pods with a sprinkle of sea salt – £2.99
- Crispy Gyoza Dumplings – dumplings filled with pork or vegetables, served with soy dipping sauce – £4.49

Beverages

- Apple Juice – freshly squeezed apple juice – £1.99
- Fruit Punch – a refreshing blend of tropical fruit juices – £2.49

Next, I asked, 'Provide "chilli challenge" maths questions (i.e. mild, medium, spicy) for children to solve based on the menu. Provide the answers at the bottom.'

Mild (miso) chilli challenge:

1 If you order the Mini Ramen Bowl for £5.99 and a glass of Apple Juice for £1.99, how much will your meal cost in total?

2 You decide to add a side of Crispy Gyoza Dumplings for £4.49 to your Mini Okonomiyaki Pancake, which costs £7.49. How much will your meal cost now?

Medium (teriyaki) chilli challenge:

3 You order Teriyaki Chicken Bites for £6.49 and a Fruit Punch for £2.49. If you give the cashier a £10 note, how much change should you receive?

4 If your friend orders a Bento Box for £9.99 and you order the same, how much will the total bill be for both of you?

Spicy (wasabi) chilli challenge:

5 Your family orders 2 Cute Sushi Rolls for £8.49 each, a plate of Sweet Mochi Ice Cream for £4.99, and 4 glasses of Apple Juice for £1.99 each. What is the total cost of the meal?

6 You have a budget of £10 to spend on your meal. If you order the Crispy Tempura Shrimp for £7.99 and a side of Edamame Pods for £2.99, will you stay within your budget? If not, how much over budget will you be?

Answers:

1 £7.98

2 £11.98

3 £1.02

4 £19.98

5 £29.93

6 You will be 98p over budget.

AI can easily provide a more complicated version of the menu and more difficult questions if you want to provide further challenge for your pupils.

32. Active Learning on Shape

Although the shape part of the maths curriculum should lend itself well to active learning, your school may or may not have good resources to use. I decided to see what AI would come up with ...

Prompt: 'Plan an active lesson on shape for 9-year-olds.'

Exploring Shapes Through Movement

Objective: To help pupils identify and understand different shapes through physical activities and interactive learning.

Materials:

- Cones
- Hula hoops
- Coloured tape
- Music player

Duration: Approximately 45–60 minutes

1 Introduction – shapes scavenger hunt (10 minutes):

- Begin the lesson by gathering the pupils in a circle.
- Show them various 2D shapes (circle, square, triangle, rectangle) and briefly discuss their characteristics.
- Explain that they are going on a scavenger hunt to find shapes around the classroom or school grounds.
- Divide the class into small teams and give each team a list of shapes to find. Provide each team with a cone or hula hoop to mark the shapes they find.

2 Shape freeze dance activity (15 minutes):

- Create shape cards with images of different shapes and place them around the activity area.
- Play upbeat music and have the pupils dance around the area.
- When the music stops, hold up a shape card. The pupils must quickly form themselves into that shape and hold it until the music resumes.

- Repeat with different shapes and encourage creativity in how they interpret and form the shapes.

3 Shape obstacle course activity (15 minutes):

- Set up an obstacle course using cones, hula hoops, and coloured tape on the ground.
- Assign each obstacle a specific shape. For instance, pupils might jump into a hula hoop (circle), crawl under a rectangle made with tape, and jump over a cone (triangle).
- Guide the pupils through the obstacle course one at a time or in small groups, encouraging them to call out the shape they are interacting with.

4 Shape art activity (10 minutes):

- Provide each pupil with a large sheet of paper and a variety of coloured markers or crayons.
- Call out a shape, and the pupils must incorporate that shape into a drawing. For example, if you say 'square', they might draw a house with square windows or a robot with a square body.
- Encourage them to think creatively while incorporating the shapes into their drawings.

5 Conclusion – shape show and tell (5 minutes):

- Gather the pupils in a circle once again.
- Have each pupil share their favourite shape from the lesson and describe how they interacted with it during the activities.
- Summarise the key concepts learned during the lesson, emphasising the different shapes they explored and how they engaged with them through movement.

Homework extension (optional):

- Ask pupils to find examples of different shapes in their homes or neighbourhoods. They can take photos or draw the objects they find and share them with the class during the next lesson.

Remember to adjust the activities based on the size of your class and the available space. The goal is to make the lesson interactive and fun while helping pupils grasp the concept of shapes in an active and engaging manner.

33. Active Maths Lessons for Abstract Concepts

Active maths is important for children because it makes abstract concepts tangible and relatable, fostering deeper understanding, engagement, and the practical application of mathematical skills in real-life situations. However, as primary maths progresses, it can become more challenging to make it active. This is where AI can help. Let's look at converting fractions to decimals as an example.

Prompt: 'Can you give me an active maths lesson on converting fractions into decimals?'

Converting Fractions to Decimals

Objective: By the end of this lesson, pupils will be able to convert fractions into decimals using division and understand the relationship between fractions and decimals.

Materials:

- Whiteboard and markers
- Fraction and decimal cards (create cards with various fractions written on them)
- Calculator (optional, for advanced examples)
- Playdough or building blocks (optional, for a hands-on activity)

Duration: Approximately 45–60 minutes

1 Introduction:

- Begin by asking the pupils if they know what fractions and decimals are. Briefly explain that fractions represent parts of a whole, while decimals are a different way to express numbers.
- Share real-world examples where decimals are used, such as money (pounds and pence) and measurements (length, weight, etc.).
- State the lesson objective and let the pupils know that they will be learning how to convert fractions into decimals.

2 Fraction and decimal match activity:

- Distribute the fraction and decimal cards to the pupils.
- In pairs or small groups, have the pupils match each fraction card with its corresponding decimal card.

- As a class, discuss the matches and ask pupils to explain their choices.

3 Interactive whiteboard demonstration activity:

- Write a few fractions on the whiteboard (e.g. ½, ¾, ⅖) and ask pupils how they can convert these fractions into decimals.
- Walk the pupils through the process of dividing the numerator by the denominator to get the decimal equivalent. For instance, for ½, you would divide 1 by 2 to get 0.5.
- Have a pupil come up to the board and demonstrate converting a fraction into a decimal.

4 Hands-on converting activity:

- Provide each pupil or group with playdough or building blocks.
- Give them a fraction (e.g. ⅜) and ask them to divide the playdough or blocks into equal parts to represent the numerator and denominator.
- After physically dividing the playdough or blocks, show pupils a pictorial representation of the fraction (with the numerator shaded). Now, have pupils count how many parts are shaded (numerator) and divide that by the total number of parts (denominator) to find the decimal equivalent.

5 Practice problems activity:

- Distribute worksheets with fraction-to-decimal conversion problems. Include a mix of simple fractions and more complex ones.
- Allow pupils to work individually or in pairs to solve the problems.
- Review the answers as a class, encouraging pupils to share their methods and explaining any misconceptions.

6 Conclusion:

- Summarise the key points of the lesson: fractions can be converted to decimals by dividing the numerator by the denominator.
- Emphasise the real-world applications of converting fractions to decimals, such as in measurements and calculations.
- Encourage pupils to practise converting fractions to decimals in their spare time and offer additional resources for practice.

Assessment:

- Assess pupils' understanding through their participation in class activities, explanations during the whiteboard demonstration, and accuracy in solving practice problems.

This active lesson plan aims to engage pupils through interactive activities, discussions, and hands-on experiences, helping them to grasp the concept of converting fractions to decimals effectively.

Of course, AI can generate lots of questions for children to solve after they have grasped the concepts through active learning.

Prompt: 'Give me 10 maths questions for 11-year-olds converting fractions to decimals with answers.'

1 Convert ½ to a decimal.

Answer: 0.5

2 Convert ¾ to a decimal.

Answer: 0.75

3 Convert ⅖ to a decimal.

Answer: 0.4

4 Convert ¼ to a decimal.

Answer: 0.25

5 Convert ³⁄₁₀ to a decimal.

Answer: 0.3

6 Convert ⅔ to a decimal.

Answer: 0.67 (rounded to two decimal places)

7 Convert ⁴⁄₇ to a decimal.

Answer: 0.57 (rounded to two decimal places)

8 Convert ⅜ to a decimal.

Answer: 0.38 (rounded to two decimal places)

9 Convert ⅕ to a decimal.

Answer: 0.2

10 Convert ²⁄₉ to a decimal.

Answer: 0.22 (rounded to two decimal places)

34. Generating Maths Strategies

When I was at school, we were taught division in a very traditional way; as a dyslexic child, I really struggled. There are now various strategies to ensure children become familiar with key concepts like share and divide, which I believe would have helped me to better understand this tricky topic. AI can give you lots of different strategies ...

Prompt: 'Tell me different division strategies.'

1 Long division: This is a traditional method where the dividend is divided by the divisor step by step, with each step involving multiplication, subtraction, and bringing down the next digit. It is suitable for dividing larger numbers.

2 Chunking (repeated subtraction): In this method, you subtract the divisor from the dividend multiple times until you can't subtract any more. The number of times you subtract is the quotient.

3 Partial quotients: Similar to chunking, this method involves breaking down the dividend into smaller chunks, subtracting multiples of the divisor, and adding up the partial quotients to get the final answer.

4 Short division: This is similar to long division but is a more compact method, suitable for simpler division problems.

5 Equal sharing (fair share): Commonly used with fractions, this method involves dividing a quantity equally among a certain number of groups.

6 Array model: This method involves representing the division problem using arrays of objects. It helps to visualise how the dividend is split into equal groups.

7 Repeated addition (multiplicative comparison): Instead of directly dividing, you can keep adding the divisor to itself until you reach or exceed the dividend, counting the number of times you add as the quotient.

8 Skip counting: You can use skip counting by the divisor to find how many times it can fit into the dividend.

9 Number line: A number line can be used to represent the division problem visually, helping to understand the process of sharing or grouping.

10 Estimation and adjusting: If the numbers are large or complex, you can estimate the answer and then adjust based on the remainder to get a more accurate quotient.

You can select different division strategies based on the complexity of the problem, personal preference, and the mathematical concepts you want to emphasise. If you are unsure about any of the techniques, give a further prompt – for example, 'Can you show me an example of the seventh strategy?'

Divide 24 by 3 using the repeated addition strategy.

Repeated addition method:

Start at zero and add the divisor (3) repeatedly until the sum reaches or exceeds the dividend (24). In this case:

$0 + 3 = 3$

$3 + 3 = 6$

$6 + 3 = 9$

$9 + 3 = 12$

$12 + 3 = 15$

$15 + 3 = 18$

$18 + 3 = 21$

$21 + 3 = 24$

Count the number of additions.

Count how many times you added the divisor. In this case, you added it 8 times.

So, when you added 3, you had to repeat it 8 times to reach the dividend 24. Therefore, 24 divided by 3 equals 8.

35. Teaching Data

You can heighten your pupils' engagement with data if you teach using topics that intrigue them. Children are usually less concerned about the type of data and more interested in its relevance to them. AI can rapidly generate data tailored to children's interests, encouraging them to interact with the subject matter while also saving you valuable time.

For example, you could ask, 'Give me data children could turn into a graph about favourite footballers.'

Footballer	Number of votes
Lionel Messi	42
Cristiano Ronaldo	35
Neymar Jr	28
Kylian Mbappé	21
Mohamed Salah	18
Harry Kane	15
Robert Lewandowski	12
Sergio Ramos	9
Kevin De Bruyne	8
Paul Pogba	6

The children could use this data to create a bar graph to visually represent the footballers and the number of votes they received.

As you can see, AI has defaulted to male players, but you can easily prompt: 'Change the above to female players from the Lionesses.'

Footballer	Number of votes
Lucy Bronze	38
Ellen White	32
Steph Houghton	26
Nikita Parris	19
Fran Kirby	15
Jill Scott	12
Beth Mead	9
Rachel Daly	7
Mary Earps	6
Georgia Stanway	5

You could then prompt: 'Generate interpretation questions based on the above data.'

1   Which female footballer received the highest number of votes as a favourite?

2   Who is the second most popular female footballer according to the votes?

3   How many more votes did Lucy Bronze receive compared to Georgia Stanway?

4   Which footballer received the least number of votes?

5   If you add up the votes for the top three female footballers, what is the total?

6   Which three footballers received more than 20 votes each?

7   Which female footballer received exactly 12 votes?

8   If you combine the votes for Fran Kirby and Jill Scott, how many votes do they have in total?

9   How many more votes did Ellen White receive compared to Beth Mead?

10 Who are the top three favourite female footballers according to the votes?

Questions like these can help children to engage with data and practise interpreting information from a dataset.

36. Teaching Coding

I really enjoy teaching coding to pupils and there are many advantages for children in learning it – for example, the development of computational thinking skills, problem-solving, logical reasoning, and the deconstruction of intricate tasks into more manageable steps. These competencies have relevance across many aspects of life and contribute to the enhancement of critical thinking skills. Coding fosters creativity and innovation, affording children the means to manifest their own concepts through programming. They can learn to create their own games, animations, narratives, and interactive projects, thereby nurturing their imagination.

Mastery of coding requires the assimilation and application of logical and sequential thought processes. Children become adept at structuring their ideas, thinking ahead, and executing tasks methodically. This systematic approach has utility in academic domains and everyday problem-solving scenarios. Coding instils a growth mindset by virtue of its inherent trial-and-error nature, encouraging children to persevere through debugging and troubleshooting. These experiences cultivate resilience.

Coding is relevant in various industries. Early exposure to coding equips children with invaluable skills that will benefit them in their future careers, opening up avenues in technology, engineering, science, and an array of other fields.

There are many free online platforms to facilitate the teaching of coding. Personally, I favour Scratch.[2] However, learning to use this platform takes time, especially for those unaccustomed to coding. An AI app offers a quick solution for generating well-structured coding lessons, which will make life easier for the uninitiated.

Prompt: 'Can you plan me an introductory lesson on coding using scratch.mit.edu?'

Introduction to Coding with Scratch

Objective: The objective of this lesson is to introduce pupils to the basics of coding and computational thinking using Scratch, an online visual programming language.

Duration: 60 minutes

Materials:

- Computers or laptops with internet access

2 See https://scratch.mit.edu.

- Scratch accounts for each pupil (if possible)

Lesson plan:

1 Introduction (5 minutes):

- Begin the lesson by explaining what coding is and its importance in today's digital world.
- Discuss how coding is used to create websites, apps, games, and more.
- Share examples of popular applications and games that were created using coding.

2 Introduction to Scratch (10 minutes):

- Introduce Scratch as a visual programming language that allows users to create interactive projects.
- Show pupils the Scratch website (scratch.mit.edu) and briefly explain its features.
- Demonstrate how to create a new project and navigate the Scratch interface.

3 Exploring Scratch (15 minutes):

- Allow pupils to explore Scratch individually or in pairs.
- Encourage them to click on different sprites, backgrounds, and blocks to see how they work.
- Ask pupils to experiment with dragging and connecting blocks to create simple animations or movements.

4 Guided activity – creating a simple animation (20 minutes):

- Guide pupils through the process of creating a simple animation using Scratch.
- Start by selecting a sprite and a background for the animation.
- Demonstrate how to use motion blocks to make the sprite move or glide across the screen.
- Introduce the 'wait' block to control the timing of the animation.
- Encourage pupils to be creative and experiment with different movements and timings.

5 Sharing and reflection (10 minutes):

- Provide time for pupils to share their animations with the class.

- Discuss what they learned during the activity and any challenges they faced.
- Ask pupils to reflect on the importance of sequencing and precise instructions in coding.

6   Extension activity (optional, depending on time):

- If time permits, provide an extension activity where pupils can explore additional features of Scratch or create a more complex project.

7   Conclusion (5 minutes):

- Recap the key concepts covered in the lesson, such as coding, Scratch, and the importance of sequencing and instructions.
- Emphasise the creativity and problem-solving skills that can be developed through coding.

Note: It is recommended to have Scratch accounts set up for each pupil prior to the lesson to save time. If not possible, pupils can still explore Scratch as guests.

Scratch involves using coloured 'blocks' as the codes to move sprites. AI can provide you with further information on these elements and explain how to use them. So, something that can be time-consuming to learn prior to teaching can be simplified with AI.

37. Science Lessons

AI can prove incredibly useful when designing science lessons. Naturally, your lesson will depend on the materials you have available. While it would be great to have a steady supply of functional miniature lightbulbs (and to not have to purchase your own batteries), regrettably, this is not always the case. However, AI can produce a wide array of ideas based on what resources you do have at your disposal.

Suppose you intend to conduct a lesson on solubility. By posing a query such as, 'What are some every-day, cost-effective soluble materials?' you can swiftly compile a list encompassing items like salt, sugar, and coffee. You can then enlist the assistance of AI to devise a lesson plan focused on your needs. A simple request like, 'Please generate a science lesson plan on solubility suitable for a 7-year-old' can yield some well-structured lesson ideas.

Discovering Solubility

Objective: To introduce the concept of solubility and explore the solubility of different materials in water.

Duration: 45 minutes

Materials:

- Clear cups or containers
- Water
- Various materials to test for solubility (e.g. salt, sugar, sand, baking soda, coffee grounds, oil)
- Stirrers or spoons
- Paper and pencils for recording observations

1 Introduction (5 minutes):

- Begin by asking the pupils if they have ever mixed something in water and observed it disappear or change. Discuss their experiences and observations.
- Explain that in today's lesson they will learn about solubility, which is the ability of a substance to dissolve in another substance, such as how sugar dissolves in water.

2 Demonstration (10 minutes):

- Choose one material, such as salt or sugar, and demonstrate its solubility by adding it to a cup of water and stirring until it dissolves.
- Discuss the changes observed, such as the material disappearing and the water changing colour or taste.

3 Activity (20 minutes):

- Divide the pupils into small groups and provide each group with cups, water, and a selection of different materials to test for solubility.
- Instruct the pupils to add a small amount of each material to separate cups of water and stir to observe if it dissolves or remains visible.
- Encourage them to record their observations, noting which materials dissolve and which do not.

4 Discussion and conclusion (10 minutes):

- Bring the pupils back together as a whole group and discuss their findings. Ask questions such as:
  - Which materials dissolved in water? Which did not?
  - Did any materials dissolve partially?
  - Did any materials change the colour or taste of the water?
- Explain that materials that dissolve completely in water are called soluble, while those that do not dissolve are called insoluble.
- Summarise the concept of solubility and its importance in various everyday situations, such as cooking or cleaning.

5 Safety tips:

- Remind pupils not to taste any of the materials used in the experiment unless instructed to do so.
- Supervise the use of stirring utensils to prevent spills or accidents.

Remember to keep the lesson engaging and interactive, allowing pupils to explore and make their own observations about solubility. Encourage them to ask questions and discuss their findings throughout the lesson.

I like the safety tips that AI provides. It would feel patronising to hear them from a colleague but, deep down, I know that these little reminders never hurt.

38. Exploring Outer Space

Real-world events can serve as potent tools for engagement, particularly for primary school teachers. Staying abreast of unfolding scientific events can be time-consuming, which is where AI can step in to assist. For instance, when planning for teaching about science or space, you can enter a question like, 'Tell me about common astronomical phenomena I could observe from Scotland and when they are likely to occur.'

1 Meteor showers:

- Perseids: Renowned as one of the most spectacular meteor showers, it reaches its zenith around 11–13 August annually. This phenomenon offers a mesmerising display featuring numerous luminous meteors gracing the sky each hour.

- Geminids: This meteor shower culminates around 13–14 December and is celebrated for generating a substantial number of meteors. It ranks among the year's most illustrious meteor showers.

- Quadrantids: This event transpires on approximately 3–4 January, characterised by an intense but relatively brief period of heightened meteor activity. Best observed during the predawn hours.

2 Lunar eclipses:

- Lunar eclipses manifest when Earth's shadow envelops the moon.

- Stay attuned to astronomical event calendars for updates on upcoming lunar eclipses visible from Scotland.

3 Solar eclipses:

- Solar eclipses materialise when the moon interposes itself between Earth and the sun, resulting in the casting of a shadow on our planet.

- These occurrences are less frequent, and their observability can differ significantly based on the specific geographic location.

4 Planetary conjunctions:

- Jupiter and Saturn conjunction: An exceptional event transpired in December 2020, when Jupiter and Saturn engaged in a rare 'great conjunction', rendering them visibly close. While such conjunctions are relatively infrequent, they continue to occur with significant intervals.

- Additional planet conjunctions (e.g. Venus and Mars) also offer captivating sights, although their occurrences vary.

5 Opposition of outer planets:

- Jupiter: At the time of its opposition, Jupiter is situated at its closest point to Earth, ensuring its visibility throughout the night. This typically transpires around May.
- Saturn: Much like Jupiter, Saturn reaches its opposition approximately in June, rendering it an opportune period to observe its enchanting rings and moons.

6 Auroras (northern lights):

- The northern lights are an outcome of solar activity interacting with Earth's magnetic field. Scotland, particularly its northern regions, can witness these captivating displays during phases of heightened solar activity.
- The prime aurora season is centred around the equinoxes in March and September, when geomagnetic activity is more probable.

7 Constellations and the Milky Way:

- As the year progresses, diverse constellations and the Milky Way grace the firmament, contingent upon the season. Winter unveils constellations like Orion and other prominent winter patterns, while the Milky Way illuminates summer nights.

It is imperative to acknowledge that while certain events adhere to specific annual dates, factors such as weather conditions, light pollution, and local topography exert an influence on visibility.

When planning learning and teaching related to outer space, it is prudent to interweave them with phenomena that pupils may potentially glimpse (or at least try to glimpse). Furthermore, children learning that weather can impede the visibility of these occurrences is a valuable lesson in its own right.

Of course, space is another curricular area where AI can help with lesson planning. To use one of the Curriculum for Excellence benchmarks as an example: 'Plan a lesson on this benchmark – Reports collaboratively on the key features of the planets including size, distance from the sun, length of day, length of year, temperature, materials from which they are predominantly made and the number of moons.'[3]

Exploring the Planets – Collaborative Reporting on Key Features

Grade level: Years 5–7 (age 9–12)

Objective: Pupils will collaboratively research and report on the key features of the planets, including size, distance from the sun, length of day, length of year, temperature, materials from which they are predominantly made, and the number of moons.

Materials:

- Chart paper or whiteboard
- Markers or coloured pencils
- Internet access or library resources
- Printed worksheets with guiding questions (optional)

Procedure:

1 Introduction (5 minutes):

   - Begin the lesson by engaging pupils in a discussion about the solar system and the planets.
   - Ask pupils what they already know about the planets and their features.
   - Explain that today, they will be working collaboratively to research and report on the key features of each planet.

2 Group formation (5 minutes):

   - Divide the class into small groups of three or four pupils.
   - Encourage diverse groupings to promote collaboration and sharing of ideas.

3 Research and reporting (30 minutes):

   - Provide each group with access to resources such as books, websites, or printed materials about the planets.

3   Education Scotland, *Benchmarks: Sciences* (March 2017), p. 17. Available at: https://education.gov.scot/media/kosdrlaj/sciencesbenchmarkspdf.pdf.

- Instruct pupils to research and gather information on the key features of each planet, focusing on size, distance from the sun, length of day, length of year, temperature, materials from which they are predominantly made, and the number of moons.

- Encourage pupils to take notes or use printed worksheets with guiding questions to organise their findings.

4 Collaborative reporting (20 minutes):

- Ask each group to choose a planet they will report on.

- Provide chart paper or a whiteboard for each group.

- Instruct pupils to collaboratively create a visual representation of their chosen planet, including the key features they researched.

- Encourage creativity and the use of colours, labels, and illustrations to make their reports visually appealing.

5 Presentations (15 minutes):

- Give each group an opportunity to present their planet report to the class.

- Encourage pupils to explain the key features they researched and answer any questions from their peers.

- As a class, discuss similarities and differences between the planets based on the reports.

6 Reflection and discussion (10 minutes):

- Lead a class discussion on what pupils learned about the planets and their key features.

- Ask pupils to share any surprises or interesting facts they discovered during the research process.

- Discuss the importance of collaboration and teamwork in completing the task successfully.

7 Extension activity (optional):

- As an extension, pupils can create a mini-booklet or poster summarising the key features of all the planets.

- Encourage pupils to include illustrations, fun facts, and memorable details to make their creations engaging.

Assessment:

- Observe pupils' engagement and participation during the research and reporting process.

- Evaluate the accuracy and completeness of their reports.

- Assess pupils' ability to present their findings clearly and answer questions from their peers.

Note: Adjust the time allocated for each section based on the needs and abilities of your pupils.

39. Religious Education

Religious education represents an aspect of the curriculum where we might naturally find ourselves in our comfort zone – and for good reason. RE plays a pivotal role in fostering acceptance and understanding among children, enabling them to embrace individuals they perceive as different from themselves. Given its significance, it is crucial to teach this subject well, as it contributes to the formulation of children's worldviews and values.

Recently, I was designing a series of RE lessons and decided to incorporate an element of choice for the class. I was secretly hopeful of persuading the children to opt for my favourite RE topic, Hinduism. I envisioned presenting it in a compelling manner which would sway the pupils towards my first choice (we have all done this, right?). However, unbeknown to me, a class library book on world religions had become popular among the pupils and a favourite RE topic had already developed in the class – Shinto.

Of course, I did what a teacher does and planned a block of lessons on Shinto. However, I lacked my usual arsenal of readily available lesson plans and resources on this topic. Consequently, I embarked on some comprehensive research to gather insights and materials on the subject. In hindsight, I could have saved myself a lot of time had I employed an AI app for assistance.

When I ask AI to create a lesson plan to introduce children to Shinto, it generates the following lesson.

Exploring Shinto: Japan's Indigenous Religion

Objective: To introduce children to the basic concepts and practices of Shinto, fostering an understanding and appreciation for Japan's indigenous religion.

Materials:

- Pictures or illustrations of Shinto shrines, kami, and nature elements
- Paper and colouring materials
- Optional: Traditional Japanese music or recordings of Shinto rituals

Lesson plan:

1 Introduction (5 minutes):
   - Begin by asking the children if they have heard of Japan or its culture.

- Explain that Japan has a unique religion called Shinto, which is an important part of Japanese culture and history.
- Show pictures or illustrations of Shinto shrines, kami, and nature elements to pique their interest.

2   What is Shinto? (10 minutes):

- Explain that Shinto is an indigenous religion of Japan.
- Discuss that Shinto focuses on the worship of kami, which are spirits or deities believed to inhabit natural elements, objects, and ancestors.
- Emphasise that Shinto is more of a way of life or a set of practices rather than a strict belief system.

3   Shinto practices (15 minutes):

- Discuss some common Shinto practices, such as visiting shrines, making offerings, and participating in purification rituals.
- Explain that Shinto rituals often involve bowing, clapping, and praying to show respect to the kami.
- Optional: Play traditional Japanese music or recordings of Shinto rituals to create a sensory experience.

4   Nature and harmony (10 minutes):

- Explain that Shinto places great importance on harmony with nature.
- Discuss how Shinto teaches respect for the natural world and the belief that kami can be found in natural elements like trees, rivers, and mountains.
- Encourage the children to share their thoughts on how they can show respect and care for nature in their own lives.

5   Colouring Shinto symbols activity (15 minutes):

- Distribute paper and colouring materials to the children.
- Provide them with colouring sheets featuring Shinto symbols like torii gates, Shimenawa ropes, or nature elements.
- Encourage them to colour in the symbols while discussing their significance.

6   Conclusion (5 minutes):

- Recap the main points discussed during the lesson.

- Ask the children if they have any questions or if there is anything they found interesting about Shinto.
- Emphasise the importance of respecting different cultures and religions.

Note: It is important to adapt the lesson plan to the age group and cultural background of the children, ensuring it is presented in an age-appropriate and respectful manner.

This lesson plan (which took seconds to devise) sparked some ideas of my own around outdoor learning: what could the children find that may have 'kami'? Was there an opportunity to tie this learning in with environmental outcomes (e.g. what have the pupils found that is living – for example, trees)? The children could then go on to learn about the role of trees in generating the oxygen we breathe, and therefore the importance of protecting them, and consider whether these ideas are in line with kami beliefs.

40. Ideas to Support Religious Observance

AI can be useful for teachers whose pupils are taking part in religious observance who would like further information or support. Religious observance often involves the whole school community, including staff, pupils, parents and faith representatives and local people.

For example, I asked an AI app, 'As a teacher, how can I support pupils who are observing Ramadan?'

Supporting pupils who are observing Ramadan involves creating an inclusive and understanding environment that accommodates their religious practices and fosters their well-being. Here are several ways you can support your pupils during Ramadan:

1. Raise awareness: At the beginning of Ramadan, educate the entire class about the significance of Ramadan and its practices. This can help to foster understanding and empathy among all pupils.

2. Flexible seating arrangements: If possible, arrange seating to accommodate pupils who might prefer to sit closer to the door or in a more private area to allow for discreet entry and exit during prayer times.

3. Flexible scheduling: If there are exams, quizzes, or other assessments, try to schedule them during times when pupils who are fasting might be more alert, such as in the morning or after they have had time to eat and rest.

4. Break fast space: Designate a quiet and private space where pupils can break their fast (if this occurs during school hours; it may during winter in some parts of the world). This area should be equipped with water and dates, which are traditionally used to break the fast.

5. Sensitivity to physical activities: Be mindful of physical activities that might be more strenuous during fasting hours. Allow alternative options or lighter activities during these times.

6. Avoid food-related activities: Be considerate when planning activities that involve food, such as cooking classes or food-related projects, during fasting hours.

7 Provide opportunities for rest: Pupils who are fasting might experience fatigue. Allow for short breaks to rest, especially during the hottest parts of the day.

8 Understanding energy levels: Be patient and understanding if pupils appear more tired or less energetic than usual. Fasting can affect energy levels, so avoid putting pressure on them to participate in activities that require a lot of physical or mental effort.

9 Flexible bathroom breaks: Allow pupils to use the bathroom when needed, as fasting can also affect hydration levels.

10 Adjustable lighting: Consider adjusting classroom lighting to create a more comfortable and restful environment for pupils who might have sensitive eyes due to fasting.

11 Emotional support: Create an open and empathetic atmosphere where pupils feel comfortable discussing any challenges they might be facing during Ramadan.

12 Cultural sensitivity: Be aware of cultural and religious sensitivities in your teaching materials, discussions, and activities.

13 Open communication: Encourage pupils to communicate their needs during Ramadan. Some pupils might need additional support, while others may not want any special attention.

14 Celebrate achievements: Recognise and celebrate the commitment and dedication of pupils who are observing Ramadan. This can boost their confidence and motivation.

15 Collaborate with families: Reach out to parents or guardians to better understand their child's needs during Ramadan and how you can offer support.

Remember that the level of support needed might vary among pupils. It is important to approach each pupil individually and with respect for their preferences and privacy. By creating an inclusive and empathetic classroom environment, you will be helping pupils to feel supported and valued during Ramadan.

41. Stories from World Religions

When teaching younger children about different faiths, it is often more engaging for them to learn stories from the religion. This approach provides a pleasant introduction that can be further developed as they grow older. Stories are a primary way through which children learn, especially when encountering new and intricate concepts.

Prompt: 'Tell me a children's story from Sikhism.'

The Kindness of Bhai Kanhaiya

Once upon a time, in the beautiful land of Punjab, there lived a man named Bhai Kanhaiya. He was a devoted follower of Guru Gobind Singh Ji, the tenth Sikh Guru. Bhai Kanhaiya was known throughout the community for his compassion and kindness.

One day, Guru Gobind Singh Ji called Bhai Kanhaiya to him and gave him a special mission. The Guru handed him a flask filled with water and a few bandages. Guru Ji said, 'Bhai Kanhaiya, take this flask of water and these bandages. Go into the battlefield and help anyone who is injured, regardless of whether they are Sikh or enemy.'

Bhai Kanhaiya nodded and set off on his mission. He went to the battlefield where a fierce battle was raging between the Sikh soldiers and the enemy forces. Amidst the chaos and fighting, Bhai Kanhaiya started serving water to the wounded soldiers and tending to their injuries.

Both Sikh and enemy soldiers were surprised by his actions. The Sikhs were grateful for his help, but some of them questioned why he was helping the enemy soldiers as well. Bhai Kanhaiya simply smiled and continued his work, offering water and care to anyone who needed it.

Word spread about Bhai Kanhaiya's selfless actions on the battlefield. Guru Gobind Singh Ji heard about his deeds and summoned him again. Guru Ji asked, 'Bhai Kanhaiya, I have heard that you are helping both our own soldiers and the enemies. Can you explain your actions?'

Bhai Kanhaiya replied respectfully, 'Guru Ji, I see all beings as part of one divine creation. When I look at them, I see the same light of the Divine in everyone. It is my duty to serve and show kindness to all, without discrimination.'

Guru Gobind Singh Ji smiled and said, 'Bhai Kanhaiya, you have truly understood the essence of Sikhism. Your service is an example for all of us. Continue to show kindness and compassion to all living beings.'

And so, Bhai Kanhaiya's acts of kindness and compassion became an inspiration for people far and wide. His story teaches us the importance of treating everyone with love and respect, regardless of their background or beliefs. It reminds us of the universal message of Sikhism: to see the divine light in all and to serve humanity selflessly.

This is a lovely story for children to reflect on and there is potential to apply it to their own lives – for example, with rival sporting teams. Other activities could include retelling the story, drawing pictures and so on.

42. Exploring Lesser Known Religions

AI can be used to help teach about lesser known or understood religions such as paganism. This is important for fostering understanding, respect, and tolerance for others.

Prompt: 'Can you plan me an introductory lesson on paganism for 7-year-olds?'

Exploring Nature and Paganism

Objective: Introduce young learners to the basic concepts of paganism, focusing on its connection to nature.

Duration: Approximately 30–40 minutes

Materials:

- Picture of nature scenes (forests, animals, flowers)
- Small stones or crystals
- Craft supplies (paper, markers, crayons)
- Storybook about nature or pagan themes (e.g. *The Lost Spells* by Robert Macfarlane and Jackie Morris, a beautiful book of poems and illustrations which can help to foster a love and appreciation of the natural world)

1 Introduction:

- Begin by showing the children pictures of beautiful nature scenes. Ask them what they notice about the pictures and what they like about nature.

2 Discussion:

- Explain that today they will learn about a special way of thinking about nature called paganism. Paganism is a belief where people see the Earth and nature as very important.

3 Nature exploration:

- Have a conversation about different things found in nature – trees, flowers, animals, rocks, etc. Ask the children to share their favourite things in nature.
- Give each child a small stone or crystal. Explain that pagans often use these special items to help them feel connected to nature.

4   Nature drawing:

- Provide craft supplies and ask the children to draw or colour a picture of something they love in nature. Encourage them to use their imagination.

5   Storytime:

- Read a short storybook or poem about nature or pagan themes (*The Lost Spells* is a good option as it focuses on the beauty of nature).

6   Discussion:

- After the story or poem, ask the children what they learned from it. Encourage them to share how it made them feel about nature.

7   Closing:

- Gather the children in a circle and have them share one thing they love about nature. Encourage them to hold their stones or crystals while sharing.

8   Reflection and home activity:

- Ask the children to think about one thing they can do to take care of nature, like picking up litter or planting a tree. Encourage them to share their ideas with their families.

Note: Remember to keep the lesson simple, interactive, and engaging for 7-year-olds. Use age-appropriate language and encourage them to share their thoughts and feelings throughout the lesson. It is also a good idea to be respectful of diverse beliefs and backgrounds within the classroom.

43. PE Lessons

During initial teacher training, trainees receive some guidance on how to teach PE; however, very few of us are experts in every type of sport. AI apps can swiftly generate detailed lesson plans on various sports, although it is advisable to specify the age group of the children. Whether it is tennis, football, rugby, or running, AI can offer suggestions for warm-ups and cool-downs too. It can be enjoyable to involve the children in the planning process – for instance, during ICT lessons, you could challenge them to use AI to create fun warm-up games for a PE lesson.

Here is an example of an AI-devised hocky lesson from the prompt: 'Plan me a hockey lesson for 10-year-olds.'

Hockey: Beginners Lesson

Objective: To introduce basic hockey skills and improve overall coordination and teamwork.

Duration: 60 minutes

1 Warm-up (10 minutes):

- Jogging: Start with a light jog around the field to warm up the muscles.
- Dynamic stretches: Perform dynamic stretches such as high knees, butt kicks, and leg swings to further warm up the body.
- Ball dribbling: Have the players dribble a hockey ball around cones, focusing on control and coordination.

2 Skill development (30 minutes):

- Stickhandling: Teach the proper technique of stickhandling, emphasising control, and close ball control. Have players practise dribbling the ball through cones or in a designated area.
- Passing and receiving: Demonstrate proper passing and receiving techniques. Have players practise passing and receiving the ball with a partner, focusing on accuracy and timing.
- Shooting: Teach the basic shooting technique, including body positioning, grip, and follow-through. Allow players to practise shooting at a target or into a goal.

3 Game/drills (15 minutes):

- Mini-game: Divide the players into two teams and play a small-sided game (3 vs 3 or 4 vs 4) to encourage teamwork and application of the skills learned.
- Relay race: Set up a relay race where players have to dribble the ball around cones, pass it to the next player, and continue until the last player shoots at a target.

4 Cool-down (5 minutes):

- Light jogging: Have the players jog lightly to gradually lower their heart rate.
- Static stretches: Guide the players through static stretches, focusing on the major muscle groups used during the session.

5 Safety tips:

- Ensure players wear appropriate protective gear, including helmets, shin guards, and mouthguards.
- Emphasise the importance of fair play and sportsmanship.
- Provide clear instructions and demonstrations for each skill to prevent injuries.

Remember to adapt the lesson plan based on the skill level and needs of the players. Have fun and encourage active participation and enjoyment throughout the session!

44. Art Lessons

AI can be an excellent resource for planning art lessons, especially when seeking suggestions to emphasise the seven core elements – line, shape, form, colour, texture, space, and value. Personally, art was one of the aspects on which I would have liked more guidance during my initial teacher training, so if you don't feel particularly confident in the realm of art, AI is your friend.

Let's consider the element of texture as an example. Prompt: 'Plan me an art lesson on texture for 8-year-olds.'

Art: Introducing the Element of Texture

Objective: To introduce the concept of texture in art and explore different ways to create texture in a tactile artwork.

Duration: 60 minutes

Materials:

- Drawing paper
- Pencils
- Crayons or coloured pencils
- Various textured materials (e.g. sandpaper, fabric scraps, bubble wrap, aluminium foil, cotton balls, feathers)
- Glue
- Scissors

1 Introduction (5 minutes):

- Begin by discussing the concept of texture with the pupils. Explain that texture refers to the way something feels or looks like it would feel if touched.
- Show examples of artworks that have different textures, such as paintings with visible brushstrokes or sculptures with rough surfaces.

2 Demonstration (10 minutes):

- Demonstrate different ways to create texture in an artwork. Show the pupils how to use different materials to make imprints or rubbings, such as pressing a textured fabric that has been painted onto paper or using a pencil to create hatching or cross-hatching lines.

3   Activity (35 minutes):

- Distribute the drawing paper to each pupil.

- Provide a variety of textured materials for the pupils to explore. Encourage them to touch and feel the materials to understand their textures.

- Instruct the pupils to choose a textured material and create a rubbing or imprint on their paper using crayons or coloured pencils. They can experiment with different pressures and colours to enhance the texture.

- Next, have the pupils use pencils or other drawing tools to create their own textures on the paper. They can draw lines, dots, or patterns to represent different textures.

- Once they have explored different techniques, allow the pupils to cut out shapes from the textured materials and glue them onto their artwork to add a three-dimensional element.

4   Wrap-up (10 minutes):

- Have the pupils share their artworks with the class, discussing the different textures they created and how they used the materials.

- Lead a brief discussion about the importance of texture in art and how it can add interest and depth to an artwork.

5   Safety tips:

- Ensure that the materials provided are safe for use by children and do not pose any hazards.

- Supervise the use of scissors to prevent accidents.

Remember to encourage creativity and experimentation throughout the lesson. Allow the pupils to explore and express their own ideas while learning about texture in art.

AI can quickly generate similar plans on the other six elements or based on the resources you have available – and, let's be honest, resources can be thin on the ground, so it makes sense to make best use of what we have stashed away in the cupboard.

45. AI-Enhanced Artwork

Over the years, I have worked with numerous pupils who were already viewing themselves as someone who 'can't draw' or 'can't do art'. Convincing children that art revolves around expression rather than producing a lifelike representation of an object can be challenging. However, with a text-to-image tool, even the hesitant artist can feel more self-assured in unleashing their imagination and creativity.

In today's rapidly evolving world, artists are increasingly embracing the digital realm. By discussing this with the children, you can emphasise that both digital and physical artwork hold equal artistic value. I wish I could have told my reluctant artists throughout the years that they would one day be capable of creating art using AI, and that an AI art gallery would exist in Amsterdam.[4]

AI also empowers children to explore various art forms. For instance, they could design an autumn tree using pointillism or 'as if painted with oil on canvas'. They have the freedom to add elements to the image as they progress or switch to an 'impressionist style' for a more ethereal effect. In addition, options like pixelation, 3D rendering, and palette knife styles offer exciting avenues for experimentation.

Suddenly, the opportunities for teaching art become boundless, even for children who initially lack confidence in drawing or painting.

---

4   The Dead End Gallery – see www.deadendgallery.nl.

46. Music Lessons

Music is an important part of children's education because it boosts cognitive development, nurtures creativity, and fosters emotional expression. Learning to play an instrument or sing in a choir can improve a child's memory, attention, and problem-solving skills. Moreover, music engages various parts of the brain, promoting holistic brain development and improving academic performance in subjects like maths and language.

In addition, music offers a unique avenue for children to explore their creativity. By composing melodies, experimenting with different instruments, and improvising, children learn to think unconventionally and approach challenges with innovative solutions. This creative outlet also builds their confidence, allowing them to showcase their individuality and talents.

Sadly, music specialists have become a rarity in many parts of the UK, leaving classroom teachers to do their best. You might be lucky and have a subscription to a music platform that offers lessons (many of which are excellent). Alternatively, you might find yourself in a school with limited access to such resources and a lack of quality musical instruments. This is where AI can ensure that this crucial aspect of the curriculum receives the attention it rightfully deserves.

Prompt: 'Plan a percussion music lesson for 6-year-olds that doesn't require instruments.'

Rhythmic Body Percussion Fun

Objective: Introduce young learners to basic rhythm concepts through body percussion and movement.

Duration: Approximately 30–40 minutes

Materials:

- Music with a steady beat (can be played from a device)
- Clear open space for movement
- Optional: scarves or ribbons for visual movement

1 Introduction:

- Gather the children in a circle and ask if they have ever heard music that makes them want to dance or clap their hands.

2 Warm-up – clap and snap:

- Begin with a simple warm-up. Teach the children how to clap their hands and snap their fingers to the beat of a fun song. Demonstrate and have them follow along.

3 Body percussion patterns:

- Explain that they can make their own music using their bodies. Show them different body percussion sounds: clapping hands, stomping feet, patting legs, and tapping shoulders.

- Create simple patterns using these sounds. For example: clap, clap, stomp, stomp. Encourage the children to follow along.

4 'Copy me' rhythms:

- Play a short rhythm using your body percussion. For instance, you can pat your legs twice, clap once, and stomp once.

- Have the children take turns being the leader. They can create their own rhythms, and the rest of the class will copy them.

5 Creative movement – dancing with scarves:

- If you have scarves or ribbons, distribute them to the children. Play music with a steady beat and encourage them to move and dance while holding the scarves. Ask them to follow the rhythm with their movements.

6 Freeze dance:

- Play the music again and have the children dance around freely. When the music stops suddenly, they must freeze in place like statues. Start the music again to resume dancing.

7 Cool-down – slow and fast movements:

- Play different types of music – slow and fast. Ask the children to move their bodies accordingly. During slow music, they can move in slow motion, and during fast music, they can move quickly.

8 Reflection:

- Gather the children and discuss the different body percussion sounds they learned and how they used their bodies to make music.

9   Home activity:

- Encourage the children to create their own body percussion rhythms at home. They can teach their family members or even create a mini-performance.

Note: Keep the lesson lively and interactive, allowing plenty of opportunities for the children to move and explore rhythm through their bodies. Adapt the activities based on the energy level of the group and provide positive reinforcement and encouragement throughout the lesson.

47. Colouring Sheets and Creative Activities

We all know the value of colouring sheets (especially on wet days when the children can't get outside to play). You can use AI to quickly generate colouring images, which can be customised to fit a theme or subject in which they are interested.

Simple prompts to create beautiful colouring images include: 'Create a blank mindful colouring picture of an owl,' 'Create a blank Easter bunny colouring image,' or 'Create a blank mindful Halloween colouring image.' These lovely images can be copied, pasted, and printed out to help keep everyone settled on rainy days.

48. Incorporating Song Lyrics

Music and songs are a great way to enrich learning in the primary setting, particularly to help the children memorise or reinforce information. For example, you might want to help a young class stay safe on Guy Fawkes Night, so you could ask AI to 'Write song lyrics on staying safe on Guy Fawkes Night to the tune of "Twinkle Twinkle Little Star"' (it is preferable to select songs the children are familiar with).

(Verse 1)

On Guy Fawkes Night, stars aglow,

Fireworks light up the sky's show.

But safety's key, we all know,

Let's have fun and stay in the know.

(Chorus)

Stay safe, stay safe, on this night,

Follow rules, everything's all right.

With adult's help, we take flight,

Enjoying fireworks, shining so bright.

(Verse 2)

Keep your distance, don't get too near,

Fireworks are loud, let's show we care.

Stay with grown-ups, never alone,

Safety first, through this fun we've known.

(Repeat chorus)

(Bridge)

Sparklers, they sparkle, oh so nice,

Hold them low, be wise, take advice.

Wear gloves, keep them at arm's length,

Safe and sound, enjoying each moment.

(Repeat chorus)

(Verse 3)

Animals may feel a bit scared,

Keep them indoors, show them you cared.

Pets and wildlife, let's be kind,

On Guy Fawkes Night, safety in mind.

(Repeat chorus)

(Outro)

With safety tips, we can delight,

In the magic of this night.

Guy Fawkes fun, our hearts ignite,

Stay safe and happy, till stars take flight.

(Repeat chorus)

The same approach can also be used to produce scripts for school plays (see section 68)!

49. Enterprise

Although enterprise education is optional for primary schools in the UK, many schools choose to incorporate elements into their curriculum. Incidentally, it can be an effective way for schools to raise vital funds. A simple AI app or website can give you lots of ideas and even theme them to fit in with seasonal events.

For example, 'Can you give me Christmas-themed school enterprise ideas for a class of 8–9-year-olds?'

1 Craft fair: Organise a Christmas craft fair where pupils create and sell handmade holiday crafts such as ornaments, greeting cards, and festive decorations.

2 Gift wrapping service: Offer a gift wrapping service where pupils wrap presents in creative and festive ways for a small fee. Provide a variety of wrapping paper, ribbons, and tags.

3 Holiday bake sale: Host a holiday bake sale featuring delicious treats like cookies, cupcakes, and holiday-themed snacks. Pupils can help to bake and package the goodies.

4 Christmas carol singing: Form a singing group and go carolling around the school or local neighbourhood. Collect donations for charity or school projects while spreading holiday cheer.

5 Christmas tree ornament sale: Design and create unique Christmas tree ornaments that pupils can sell. These could be personalised ornaments or themed sets.

6 Hot chocolate stand: Set up a hot chocolate stand during school events or after school hours. Offer different toppings like marshmallows and whipped cream to make it extra special.

7 Christmas storybook sale: Pupils can write and illustrate their own Christmas-themed storybooks. Compile them into booklets and sell them to parents, friends, and family.

8 Poinsettia plant sale: Coordinate with a local nursery to offer poinsettia plants for sale. These festive plants are popular during the holiday season.

9   Gingerbread house decorating kits: Create DIY gingerbread house decorating kits with pre-baked gingerbread pieces, icing, and assorted candies. These can make for fun family activities.

10 Christmas-themed art exhibition: Host an art exhibition featuring pupils' Christmas-themed artwork. You can sell prints, cards, or even auction off some pieces.

11 Elf delivery service: Offer a service where pupils dress up as elves and deliver holiday cards or small gifts to classrooms or offices within the school.

12 Christmas puzzle challenge: Design and create Christmas-themed puzzles, riddles, and brain teasers. Pupils can sell these challenges with solutions included.

Remember to involve pupils in the planning, decision-making, and implementation of these ideas to make the experience educational and enjoyable. These activities can also be used as opportunities to teach them about teamwork, budgeting, marketing, and communication skills.

50. Utilising Local History and Culture

Children find it fascinating if some of their learning is focused on the local area. Every town or village has its own unique folklore, myths, and traditions to beguile children. AI can help you to discover information about local history and plan related lessons.

I live in Renfrewshire, so an example might be: 'Tell me about local history in Paisley, Scotland.' As a resident, I think AI has done a decent job in identifying aspects of the town's history.

Paisley, located in the west of Scotland, is a town with a rich and diverse local history. Here are some key points about Paisley's history:

1 Medieval origins: Paisley's history dates back to the medieval period when it was established as a centre of religious significance. The town's name is derived from the Old British word 'passeleg' which means 'basilica' or 'church'.

2 Paisley Abbey: One of the most significant landmarks in Paisley is the Paisley Abbey. Founded in the 12th century, the abbey has played a central role in the town's history and development. It has survived various challenges over the centuries and remains a symbol of Paisley's historical and architectural heritage.

3 Textile industry: In the 18th and 19th centuries, Paisley became famous for its textile industry, particularly its production of paisley pattern shawls. These intricate and colourful designs became highly sought after and were exported all over the world. The textile industry contributed significantly to Paisley's economic growth during this period.

4 Industrial Revolution: The Industrial Revolution had a profound impact on Paisley, leading to the growth of industries such as weaving, thread-making, and cotton spinning. The town's skilled workforce and access to waterways contributed to its industrial success.

5 Sma' Shot Day: A unique cultural event in Paisley is the Sma' Shot Day, which commemorates the weavers' tradition of the 'sma' shot' – an extra thread used in the weaving process that the weavers had to pay for themselves. The event celebrates the local working-class history and involves parades, performances, and festivities.

6 Political and social history: Paisley has been a centre of political and social activism throughout its history. It was associated with figures like Thomas Coats, a philanthropist and politician who made significant contributions to the town. The town's history also includes moments of labour strikes and political movements.

7 Cultural heritage: Paisley has a vibrant cultural scene, with various museums, galleries, and cultural events. The town's history and heritage are preserved and showcased at places like Paisley Museum and Art Galleries.

8 Modern developments: In recent years, Paisley has been working on revitalising its town centre and promoting its cultural and historical attractions. The town's bid for UK City of Culture in 2021 brought attention to its rich cultural heritage.

9 Paisley witch hunts: Another significant chapter in Paisley's history is its association with witch hunts during the 17th century. Like many other parts of Europe, Paisley was not immune to the hysteria surrounding accusations of witchcraft. The witch hunts resulted in the persecution and execution of several individuals accused of practising witchcraft.

These are just a few highlights of Paisley's history. The town's evolution from its medieval roots, through its industrial heyday, to its modern cultural initiatives, showcases a dynamic history that has contributed to its identity and character.

Lots of my pupils have been intrigued by the history of the witch hunts; AI can plan great lessons on this topic.

Prompt: 'Plan me a lesson on the Paisley witch hunts for 10-year-olds.'

Unravelling the Mystery of the Paisley Witch Hunts

Grade: Years 5–6 (10–11-year-olds)

Objective:

- To introduce pupils to the historical context of the Paisley witch hunts.
- To help pupils understand the impact of historical events on a community.

- To encourage critical thinking and empathy through discussions on justice and prejudice.

Duration: 1 hour

Materials:

- Pictures of the Paisley Witches Memorial
- Printed short excerpts from historical records (simplified for comprehension)
- Large paper or whiteboard
- Markers

Lesson plan:

1 Introduction (10 minutes):

- Begin the lesson by asking pupils what they know about witches or witch hunts.
- Show pictures of the Paisley Witches Memorial and ask if anyone has seen it or knows its significance.

2 Historical context (10 minutes):

- Provide a brief overview of historical times when people believed in witches and witchcraft.
- Explain that Paisley, like many places, had its own witch hunts where people were accused of being witches.
- Mention that these hunts happened a long time ago and people had different beliefs back then.

3 Interactive reading (15 minutes):

- Hand out printed excerpts from historical records related to the Paisley witch hunts. Make sure the language is simplified for comprehension.
- Read aloud the excerpts as a class or have pupils take turns reading.
- Pause after each excerpt to discuss what the pupils understood. Ask questions like:
  - Why do you think people accused others of being witches?
  - How do you think the accused witches felt?
  - What might have caused the misunderstandings?

4   Discussion (10 minutes):

- Lead a class discussion on justice and prejudice.
- Ask pupils if they think it was fair to accuse people of being witches without strong evidence.
- Discuss how rumours and fear can lead to unfair treatment of innocent people.
- Encourage pupils to share their thoughts on what they would have done if they were living in that time.

5   Empathy activity (10 minutes):

- Divide the pupils into pairs.
- Each pair will imagine they are living in the time of the witch hunts. One pupil will take on the role of an accused witch and the other will be a supportive friend.
- Have them engage in a conversation where the friend tries to understand the feelings and fears of the accused.

6   Creative expression (5 minutes):

- Ask pupils to think about what they have learned and draw a picture that represents what they think about the Paisley witch hunts.

7   Reflection (5 minutes):

- Gather the pupils and discuss their drawings briefly.
- Ask if they feel they have learned something new and if they have any questions.

Homework (optional):

- Pupils can write a short paragraph about how they would help someone who is unfairly accused or misunderstood, drawing inspiration from the lesson.

Assessment:

- Monitor class participation during discussions and assess pupils' understanding through their drawings and written reflections (if assigned as homework).

51. Higher Order Thinking Skills

Higher order thinking skills (HOTS) are essential for children's development as they go beyond basic understanding and memorisation. These skills – including problem-solving, critical thinking, creativity, and analytical abilities – enable children to handle real-world challenges, assess information critically, and make informed decisions. They promote comprehension, effective communication, and empathy, while also preparing children for lifelong learning, independence, and adaptability. HOTS questions are great for challenging reading comprehension questions and many can be applied to multiple texts, which is a great time-saver!

Prompt: 'Generate 10 (child-friendly) higher order thinking skills questions that can be used for various texts.'

1 Critical thinking: What are the main problems faced by the characters in the story? How do they try to solve them?

2 Predictive thinking: What do you think will happen next in the story? Why do you believe that?

3 Comparative thinking: How is the main character similar to or different from you? How do these similarities or differences affect their decisions?

4 Cause and effect: Can you identify a cause-and-effect relationship in the story? How did one event lead to another?

5 Inferential thinking: What can you infer about a character's feelings based on their actions and words in the text?

6 Creative thinking: If you were the author, how would you change the ending of the story? What alternative ending can you imagine?

7 Problem-solving: If the characters faced a different challenge, how might they solve it? Would their actions be the same or different? Why?

8 Analytical thinking: What are the key events in the story, and how do they contribute to the overall plot or message?

9 Empathy and perspective: How do you think the other characters feel about the choices the main character made? Why do you think they might feel that way?

10 Summarisation: Can you summarise the story in just a few sentences while still capturing its most important aspects?

Feel free to adapt these questions to suit the specific text you are working with. They should help to engage young readers in thoughtful discussions and encourage deeper comprehension of the material.

These questions can be copied, pasted, printed, and kept for fast finishers, extension activities, or for children who require extra challenge.

52. Teaching Politics and Democracy

Political events are continually unfolding, providing opportunities to teach pupils about the concept of democracy. It is most engaging to teach this subject when an election is underway, as pupils can observe the process and watch news reports in the run-up to the event. When there aren't national or local elections, it can be beneficial to delve into political systems in Europe (especially if these tie in with other areas of the curriculum, such as modern languages) or the United States.

However, understanding different types of democratic government in depth can be challenging, to say the least. AI can offer a helping hand by providing an explanation of any political system.

Prompt: 'Can you give a child-friendly explanation of the American House of Representatives elections?'

In the United States, there is a special group of people called the House of Representatives. They are like a big team that helps make important decisions for the country. But did you know that the members of the House of Representatives are not there forever? They have to be elected by the people.

Every two years, there is a special event called an election where people get to choose who they want to represent them in the House of Representatives. It is a bit like a popularity contest, but instead of voting for the coolest person, they vote for the person they think will do the best job of representing their community.

During the election, different candidates from different political parties will try to convince people to vote for them. They might have signs, commercials, or even go door-to-door to talk to people and share their ideas. They will tell voters what they believe in and what they want to do if they get elected.

On the day of the election, people who are old enough and registered to vote can go to a special place called a polling station. There, they will be given a ballot with the names of all the candidates running for the House of Representatives. They can choose the person they think will be the best representative for their community and mark their choice on the ballot.

After the voting is done, all the votes are counted up. The candidate who gets the most votes in their district becomes the representative for that area. They will go to Washington, DC, where the House of Representatives meets, and work with other representatives to make important decisions that affect the country.

So, the House of Representatives elections are a way for the people to have a say in who represents them and makes decisions on their behalf. It is an important part of democracy in the United States and helps to make sure that everyone's voice is heard.

You may need further explanation or details, so prompt: 'Give a child-friendly explanation of how the House of Representatives and Congress work together.'

In the United States, there is a special group of people called Congress. Congress is like a big team that helps make important decisions for the country. It is made up of two parts: the House of Representatives and the Senate.

The House of Representatives is like one half of Congress. It has lots of members, and each member represents a different area of the country called a district. They are kind of like superheroes for their district because they listen to the people who live there and try to make decisions that will help them.

The House of Representatives is responsible for making and voting on laws. If someone has an idea for a new law, they have to share it with the House of Representatives. The members of the House of Representatives talk about the idea, ask questions, and decide if it should become a law. They vote on it, and if most of them say 'yes', then it goes to the next step.

The next step is where the House of Representatives and the Senate work together. The Senate is the other half of Congress, and it also has lots of members. Each state gets two senators, no matter how big or small the state is. The senators listen to the people in their state and try to make decisions that will help them too.

When the House of Representatives passes a law, it goes to the Senate. The senators also talk about the law, ask questions, and decide if it should become a law. They vote on it too, and if most of them say 'yes', then the law moves forward.

But here is the important part: both the House of Representatives and the Senate have to agree on the same version of the law. They might have different ideas or changes they want to make. So, they have to talk to each other and find a way to compromise. It is like when you and your friends want to play a game but have different rules. You have to talk and find a way to play that makes everyone happy.

Once they agree on the final version of the law, it goes to the president. The president is like the boss of the country. They can either sign the law and make it official, or they can say 'no' and veto it. If the president signs the law, it becomes a law and everyone has to follow it. But if the president vetoes it, the law doesn't become official unless the House of Representatives and the Senate can get enough votes to override the veto.

So, the House of Representatives and the Senate work together to make laws for the United States. They listen to the people they represent, talk about ideas, and vote on them. They also have to work with the president to make sure the laws become official. It is a big team effort to help the country run smoothly and make decisions that are fair for everyone.

And, of course, AI can help you to understand more complex political issues closer to home, such as the second vote in Scottish parliamentary elections. As someone who has taught Scottish democracy many times, I am quite impressed by the child-friendly explanation that AI generated on this subject.

Alright, imagine you and your friends are picking a game to play at breaktime. There are three games you all like: football, tag, and hide-and-seek. But you can only play one game today. You want to make sure the game that most of your friends like is the one you all play. So, you come up with a clever plan called the 'second vote system'.

Here's how it works: first, everyone votes for their favourite game out of the three options. Let's say six friends voted for football, four for tag, and five for hide-and-seek. Now, football got the most votes, but not everyone likes football. Some friends like tag and hide-and-seek more.

That's where the second vote comes in! Since football didn't get all the votes, you give your friends another chance to pick from the remaining two games – tag and hide-and-seek. This time, they only vote for either tag or hide-and-seek.

Now, let's say seven friends voted for tag and eight for hide-and-seek. Hide-and-seek got the most votes this time. So, you all decide to play hide-and-seek because more friends like it the most when you consider both votes.

This way, the game that most friends like wins, even if it didn't get the most votes in the first round. The second vote helps to make sure everyone's happy with the choice. Just like in Scottish elections, this system helps choose the best person to help run the country, even if they didn't get the most votes at first. It is all about making sure most people are happy with the decision in the end!

53. Addressing Dictatorship

Sticking with the concept of democracy for a little longer, we can help our children to understand democracy if we show them what the opposite looks like; children are often fascinated by dictatorships. You could enhance the learning by discussing a nation that is relevant to a current event or topic. For example, do children think that Russia's style of government may have contributed to the war on Ukraine? Could things have been different if it was safer to oppose and criticise the government? Is democracy all about elections alone?

Prompt: 'Which countries are not democracies and what systems do they have instead?'

There are several countries in the world that are not considered democracies. It is important to note that political systems can vary, and some countries may have elements of democracy alongside other governing structures. Here are a few examples:

1   China: China is governed by the Chinese Communist Party, which operates under a one-party system. The party holds significant control over the government and decision-making processes.

2   North Korea: North Korea operates under a system known as Juche, which is a form of totalitarianism. The country is ruled by the Kim dynasty, with power concentrated in the hands of the Supreme Leader.

3   Saudi Arabia: Saudi Arabia is an absolute monarchy, where the ruling monarch holds ultimate authority over the government and decision-making. The country does not have elected representatives or a democratic system.

4   Iran: Iran is an Islamic Republic. While it has elements of democracy, ultimate power rests with the Supreme Leader, who is not elected by the people. The Guardian Council, which is not directly elected, also holds significant influence over the political process.

5   Cuba: Cuba is governed by the Communist Party, which operates under a one-party system. The party holds significant control over the government and decision-making processes.

6   Russia: Russia operates under a system that has been described as an 'illiberal democracy' or 'competitive authoritarianism'. While there are elections, critics argue that the political environment is heavily influenced

by the ruling party, and opposition voices face restrictions and limitations.

7 Belarus: Belarus is often referred to as an authoritarian state, with power concentrated in the hands of President Alexander Lukashenko. The country has been criticised for its lack of political freedoms, restrictions on the media, and limited opposition participation.

It is important to note that the political landscape can be complex, and categorising countries as purely democratic or non-democratic can sometimes be challenging. Additionally, political systems can evolve and change over time.

AI can also help us to think critically about our own political system.

Prompt: 'Is the UK a true democracy?'

The United Kingdom is often considered a parliamentary democracy. It has a system where citizens elect representatives to the Parliament, and the government is formed by the political party or coalition that has the majority of seats in the House of Commons. However, it is important to note that the UK has some unique features that differentiate it from other democracies.

One aspect that distinguishes the UK is its constitutional monarchy. While the monarch's role is largely ceremonial, they still have some influence in the political process. The prime minister, who is the head of government, is appointed by the monarch and is typically the leader of the majority party in the House of Commons.

Additionally, the UK does not have a written constitution like some other democracies. Instead, it relies on a combination of statutes, common law, and constitutional conventions. This flexible and evolving system allows for a degree of parliamentary sovereignty, where the Parliament has the ultimate authority in making and changing laws.

However, it is worth noting that no democracy is perfect, and there are ongoing debates and discussions about the effectiveness and fairness of the UK's democratic processes. Some critics argue that certain aspects, such as the first-past-the-post electoral system or the unelected House of Lords, could be reformed to enhance representation and accountability.

54. Utilising Available Resources

As teachers, we all know that resources can be in short supply. AI can help you to come up with things to do with the resources you already have. For example, I have a box of ice lolly sticks in my cupboard; years from now, I still won't have used them all up in assessment for learning strategies, so I may as well do something with them!

I can ask an AI app, 'Suggest science, technology, engineering, and mathematics (STEM) activities I can do with 10-year-olds using ice lolly sticks.'

1   Structural engineering challenge: Provide ice lolly sticks and craft glue, and challenge the children to build a tall tower or a sturdy bridge using only the sticks. This activity introduces them to the basics of structural engineering and balance.

2   Geodesic dome construction: Teach children about geometry and architecture by guiding them to construct a geodesic dome using ice lolly sticks and small rubber bands. They can learn about shapes, angles, and the strength of structures.

3   Catapults: Have the children design and build mini catapults using ice lolly sticks and rubber bands. They can experiment with different designs to see how far they can launch small objects. This activity introduces basic physics concepts like force and motion.

4   Puzzles: Encourage creativity and problem-solving by having the children design their own puzzles using ice lolly sticks. They can arrange the sticks to form shapes or patterns, then challenge their friends to solve the puzzles.

5   Magnetic maze: Attach magnets to the ends of ice lolly sticks and create a maze on a flat surface using the sticks. Then, using a magnet placed underneath the surface, guide a magnetic ball through the maze, introducing children to magnetism and spatial reasoning.

6   Harmonica: Show the children how to create a simple musical instrument using ice lolly sticks and rubber bands. They can explore the science of sound and vibration as they experiment with different lengths and tensions of the rubber bands.

7   Bridge strength test: Provide weights of increasing amounts and challenge the children to build bridges using ice lolly sticks that can

support the weights without collapsing. This activity introduces concepts of load-bearing capacity and engineering design.

8   Solar system model: Help the children create a scale model of the solar system using ice lolly sticks to represent the planets and various distances. This activity combines astronomy and maths as they calculate and visualise the vastness of space.

9   Electric circuit: Teach the children about basic circuits by having them create a simple circuit using ice lolly sticks, copper tape, and a small LED light. They can learn about conductivity and how circuits work.

10 Maths puzzles: Use ice lolly sticks to create maths puzzles like equations, patterns, or shapes. Have the children solve the puzzles and discover how maths concepts can be visually represented.

Remember to provide adult supervision and adapt the activities to suit the skill level and interests of the children. These hands-on activities will not only make STEM learning enjoyable but also encourage creativity, critical thinking, and teamwork.

55. Impromptu Learning Opportunities

We all recognise the importance of adaptive planning in the primary setting. When something novel or interesting arises, it is futile to resist the children's curiosity; in fact, we should embrace the opportunities that such occurrences bring. AI can assist in formulating impromptu plans for situations like snow, storms, high winds, or any other unexpected events.

For example, 'Can you give me STEM lesson ideas about snow for young children?'

1 Snowflake observation:
- Show the children pictures of different snowflakes and discuss their unique shapes.
- Provide paper and scissors/safety scissors for the children to cut out their own paper snowflakes.
- Encourage them to notice and talk about the patterns and designs they create.

2 Melting snow science:
- Set up an experiment where the children can place snow in different containers indoors and outdoors.
- Observe and discuss which container melts the snow faster and why (e.g. warmth indoors, sunlight outdoors).
- Incorporate simple language about heat transfer and changes of state.

3 Snow measurement and maths:
- Take the children outside to gather snow and bring it indoors.
- Provide measuring cups, spoons, and containers to measure and compare the volume of snow.
- Introduce basic concepts of measurement and mathematical comparisons.

4 Snowy animal tracks:
- If there is fresh snow outside, look for animal tracks in the school grounds or a nearby park.
- Discuss the idea of animal footprints and how they leave traces in the snow.

- Use animal figures or cut-outs to make tracks in soft playdough or sand indoors.

5 Build a mini snowman:
  - Bring in a small container of snow (if available) and have the children create mini snowmen indoors.
  - Discuss shapes and sizes while they assemble their snowmen.
  - Use buttons, beads, or other small objects for eyes, nose, and buttons.

6 Snowy science art:
  - Mix watercolour paint with snow and encourage children to paint with the snowy mixture on paper.
  - Discuss the changes in colour and texture as the snow melts.
  - Incorporate elements of science (melting) and art (painting) in this activity.

7 Snow sensory exploration:
  - Provide different types of snow (wet, fluffy, compact) for the children to touch and play with.
  - Discuss how snow feels, its texture, and how it changes as they handle it.
  - Use descriptive words to encourage vocabulary development.

8 Snowy building blocks:
  - Provide building blocks, toy animals, and other small items.
  - Let the children build structures and landscapes using blocks and snow as a construction material.

9 Snowy sink or float:
  - Fill a basin with snow and collect various small objects.
  - Have the children predict whether each object will sink or float in the snow.
  - Discuss the properties of objects and how they interact with snow.

Remember to keep the activities simple, hands-on, and age appropriate. These activities can help young children to develop their curiosity, observational skills, and early STEM concepts in a fun and engaging way.

Remember, even 'bad' weather can present fun learning opportunities; AI can also suggest many simple STEM activities to do when it is raining!

56. AI to Enrich Outdoor Learning

Many AI apps include an image-to-text function that can be used to help children explore descriptive language. The possibilities for story writing and character and setting description are exciting. For example, when I enter one of my favourite photos, which I took during a snowy walk, it generates a beautiful description:

In this picturesque winter scene, a snowy path winds its way through a serene forest. The path, covered in a thick layer of pristine white snow, creates a stark contrast against the dark, towering trees that line its sides. The trees, adorned with delicate snowflakes, stand tall and proud, their branches reaching towards the sky. The air is crisp and still, as if nature itself is holding its breath in the tranquil beauty of the moment.

Alongside the path, a rustic wooden fence emerges from the snow, adding a touch of charm to the scene. The fence, weathered by time and elements, showcases its intricate craftsmanship, with each wooden plank perfectly aligned. The snow delicately blankets the fence, creating a harmonious blend of nature's elements.

As you walk along the path, the soft crunch of snow beneath your feet echoes through the stillness, creating a soothing melody. The air is filled with a faint scent of pine, as the trees release their natural fragrance into the wintry atmosphere. The occasional ray of sunlight peeks through the dense canopy, casting a gentle glow on the path, illuminating the way forward.

This enchanting winter landscape invites you to take a leisurely stroll, allowing you to immerse yourself in the tranquillity and serenity that only nature can provide. The snowy path, framed by majestic trees and adorned with a charming fence, offers a momentary escape from the hustle and bustle of everyday life, allowing you to find solace and peace in the beauty of the winter wonderland.

AI also expands the possibilities for outdoor learning. For example, when children come across captivating plants or insects, a straightforward AI phone app can furnish them with rich descriptions of their finds. For example, a photo of apples on the tree in my garden produces:

> In this vibrant image, a majestic tree stands tall and proud, adorned with a bountiful harvest of ripe, juicy apples. The tree's sturdy trunk and branches reach towards the sky, displaying a mesmerising display of nature's abundance. The leaves, painted in various shades of green, dance in the gentle breeze, creating a soothing melody as they rustle against each other. The apples, vibrant and plump, hang delicately from the branches, their vibrant reds and greens contrasting beautifully against the tree's lush foliage. Each apple seems to beckon with its lusciousness, promising a burst of sweetness with every bite. The tree, a symbol of life and sustenance, stands as a testament to the wonders of nature, inviting us to appreciate its beauty and indulge in the delicious fruits it offers.

And a photo of a rose generates:

> In this vibrant image, a stunning red rose stands proudly amidst a lush red rose bush. The rose, with its velvety petals, exudes elegance and grace, captivating all who lay eyes upon it. Its deep crimson hue is intensified by the surrounding sea of equally vibrant roses, creating a breathtaking display of nature's beauty. The rose bush, adorned with thorny branches, serves as a protective embrace for this exquisite flower, ensuring its safety and allowing it to flourish. The sunlight gently filters through the leaves, casting a warm glow upon the scene, illuminating the intricate details of each petal and highlighting the delicate fragrance that fills the air. This captivating sight evokes a sense of romance and passion, reminding us of the timeless allure and symbolism associated with the red rose.

AI's ability to integrate outdoor learning with literacy makes it a useful tool for expanding children's language skills.

57. AI-Generated Geographical Features

You can use an AI-powered text-to-image tool to illustrate various geographical features, such as a bubbling hot spring or an erupting geyser, making it an invaluable asset across the curriculum. Imagine a scenario where pupils are learning about the Earth's diverse landscapes. With the help of an AI image generator, educators can instantly conjure up visual representations of breathtaking natural wonders. These visuals not only enhance the pupils' comprehension but also spark their curiosity and imagination.

This technology bridges the gap between theoretical knowledge and real-world contexts. Pupils can delve into the fascinating science behind these natural phenomena, learning about the forces of nature that shape our planet. They can discuss the significance of these features within ecosystems as well as exploring cultural and historical connections.

Furthermore, AI-generated images can serve as creative prompts for assignments. Pupils might be inspired to craft descriptive essays, engage in research projects, or even embark on virtual journeys where they imagine themselves visiting these geographical marvels.

Incorporating AI text-to-image capabilities in education thus transforms the learning experience. It fosters a deeper understanding of subjects, fuels curiosity, and encourages interdisciplinary exploration, ultimately preparing pupils to become informed and engaged global citizens.

58. Cross-Curricular Connections

Cross-curricular teaching, also known as interdisciplinary or integrated teaching, involves the intentional blending of concepts, skills, and content from multiple subject areas within a single lesson or project. This approach offers numerous benefits that contribute to a richer and more holistic educational experience for pupils. Cross-curricular teaching can aid the development of HOTS and critical thinking, and help children learn to transfer skills and knowledge.

Cross-curricular instruction requires thoughtful planning to produce holistic, engaging, and meaningful educational experiences for pupils, so although it is very worthwhile, it can be time-consuming to produce and link ideas. If there is a topic or current event that the children are interested in, AI can easily help you to make it cross-curricular.

Prompt: 'Plan a cross-curricular topic on the Winter Olympics for 9-year-olds.'

Cross-Curricular Winter Olympics Exploration for 9-Year-Olds

Duration: 4–6 weeks (adjustable based on school schedule)

Subject integration: PE, geography, history, art, mathematics, literacy

Week 1–2 – introduction to the Winter Olympics and geography:

- PE: Introduction to winter sports featured in the Winter Olympics, such as skiing, figure skating, and snowboarding. Basic skills and rules.

- Geography: Explore the countries participating in the Winter Olympics. Research and locate these countries on maps and globes.

Week 3–4 – history and culture of the Winter Olympics:

- History: Learn about the history of the Winter Olympics. Investigate the first Winter Olympics, how it has evolved, and significant moments.

- Art: Create national flags and symbols of the countries participating. Discuss the significance of these symbols.

Week 5 – winter sports data and maths:

- Mathematics: Collect and analyse data related to winter sports events, such as the fastest skiing time or highest jump in snowboarding. Create graphs and charts to visually represent the data.

Week 6 – creative writing and closing celebration:

- Literacy: Write descriptive pieces about a chosen winter sport or a fictional story involving a winter sports adventure.
- Art: Create winter sports-themed artwork using various mediums.
- PE: Organise a mini 'Winter Olympics' event within the school. Pupils participate in adapted winter sports and compete in a friendly manner.

Assessment and evaluation:

- Participate in PE activities, demonstrating understanding of selected winter sports.
- Complete geography assignments on countries participating in the Winter Olympics.
- Share historical facts about the Winter Olympics in class presentations.
- Display understanding of data representation through maths activities.
- Showcase creative writing pieces and artwork.
- Reflect on the learning experience through discussions and written reflections.

Extensions and adaptations:

- Collaborate with the school's technology department to create multimedia presentations about different winter sports.
- Organise a multicultural food day featuring dishes from countries participating in the Winter Olympics.
- Invite guest speakers, such as former athletes or sports coaches, to share their experiences and insights with the pupils.

This cross-curricular Winter Olympics exploration engages 9-year-olds in an immersive learning experience that incorporates physical activity, cultural awareness, historical understanding, artistic expression, mathematical analysis, and language skills. It provides a well-rounded approach to learning while catering to various learning styles and interests.

59. Creating Scenes to Enhance Learning

AI text-to-image generators can be useful in bringing history to life, such as historic battles or major scientific discoveries. These tools can also be beneficial in developing children's vocabulary. You could challenge them to create a series of images that retell a religious story or describe a scene from a book; their language must be clear enough that the app recreates the scene in the way they imagine it. This can bring a novel and engaging element of virtual reality to pupils' learning.

60. Teaching Critical Thinking

I recently taught a class on recognising the difference between facts and opinions. Critical thinking skills are crucial for children because they empower them to analyse information, make well-informed decisions, solve complex problems, and navigate the challenges of an ever-changing world.

Critical thinking is an enjoyable aspect of the primary curriculum, although providing numerous examples for children to discuss and contemplate can be a slow process. However, AI can quickly produce as many examples as you need – for example, 'Can you give me 20 fact or opinion statements for children to consider (mix the statements up)?'

1   Apples are a type of fruit.

2   Dogs are the best pets.

3   The sun rises in the east.

4   Ice cream is tastier than pizza.

5   Elephants can fly.

6   Earth is the only planet with water.

7   Reading is more fun than playing video games.

8   The moon is made of cheese.

9   All birds can swim.

10 Football is the most popular sport in the world.

11 Water boils at 100 degrees Celsius.

12 Chocolate is the most delicious food.

13 Giraffes have long necks to reach leaves.

14 A tiger's stripes help it hide in the jungle.

15 The Great Wall of China can be seen from space.

16 Dinosaurs still roam the Earth.

17 The fastest land animal is the cheetah.

18 Carrots help you see in the dark.

19 Sharks are friendly creatures.

20 Rainbows are made of candy and wishes.

Encourage the children to think critically and determine whether each statement is a fact (can be proven true or false) or an opinion (based on personal feelings or beliefs).

61. AI-Generated Images to Convey Abstract Concepts

Within the science curriculum, our aim is often to help children grasp abstract concepts that are difficult to visualise – for example, magnetism, volume, or movement. AI enables us to rapidly produce a diverse array of images – anything from neurons, lungs and bacteria to the solar system, galaxies and Mars. Images not only deepen children's understanding but also ignite their curiosity and engagement, thereby facilitating a more profound understanding of these complex subjects.

62. Playground Duty

Different schools have different arrangements for breaks and lunchtimes. Whether you find yourself on playground duty or simply seeking some enjoyable outdoor games, AI can assist you. Just input 'Tell me an easy playground game' to get started.

Game: Duck, Duck, Goose

Objective: To have fun and engage in a simple group activity.

Number of players: Ideally five or more, but it can be adapted for smaller groups.

How to play:

1   Setup: Have all the players sit in a circle on the ground.

2   Select a 'goose': Choose one player to be the 'goose'. This player will stand up and walk around the outside of the circle while gently tapping each seated player on the head, saying 'duck' each time they tap.

3   Choose the 'chaser': At some point, the 'goose' will tap a player on the head and say 'goose' instead of 'duck'. The player who was tapped as the 'goose' now becomes the 'chaser'.

4   Chase and tag: The 'chaser' stands up and tries to chase down the original 'goose' as they run around the circle. The goal of the 'chaser' is to tag the 'goose' before they are able to sit down in the 'chaser's' empty spot in the circle.

5   Outcome: If the 'chaser' tags the 'goose' before they reach the empty spot, the 'goose' becomes the new 'chaser', and the game continues with the new roles. If the 'goose' successfully sits in the empty spot, the 'chaser' returns to their original spot in the circle, and the game starts over again.

6   Variations: Players can add variations by using different words in place of 'duck' and 'goose', or by introducing extra rules to make the game more exciting.

7   Ending: The game can continue for a set period or until everyone has had a chance to be the 'chaser' at least once. You can decide the ending based on the energy and interest of the players.

'Duck, duck, goose' is a great way for children to socialise, have some physical activity, and practise their motor skills in a playful manner. It is an easy and timeless game that can be played almost anywhere with enough space for a circle of players to sit and run around.

63. Pupil Research

Many pupils are already familiar with social media apps that incorporate AI features, such as Snapchat. If they are empowered to utilise AI, it can become a vital research tool for homework and other independent tasks.

AI can infuse the research process with an element of fun, encouraging pupils to explore and discover new information; in particular, it can motivate those children who are often the most reluctant to participate in homework. AI tools can help to level the playing field and make education more accessible, so it can also be beneficial for pupils who face barriers to learning.

By incorporating AI into research assignments, we can introduce pupils to essential skills early on. For instance, we can teach them about the importance of referencing by asking them to attribute the information they find via AI and provide a link to the source website. In the same way that tools like spell-checkers have become staples in the writing process, so AI can become an integral aid for learning, fostering both independence and critical thinking.

This approach can also help pupils to develop important digital literacy skills. They will learn to evaluate sources, determine the credibility of information, and effectively navigate the vast sea of online content.

So, by integrating AI, we not only make education more interactive, inclusive, and relevant, and research more efficient, but we also equip pupils with skills that are crucial in today's information-rich world. Ultimately, AI has the capacity to revolutionise the way pupils engage with knowledge.

64. Fairtrade Schools

With young people so aware of and educated about poverty being caused more by politics than bad luck, many may be inspired and motivated to work towards a Fairtrade School Award.[5] There are numerous benefits to the children, such as the learning opportunities, a feeling of empowerment, fostering a sense of global citizenship, and the potential for parental and community involvement.

AI can help by generating lots of ideas to help your pupils earn a Fairtrade award, so you can choose the ones most achievable and relevant to your setting and school community.

Prompt: 'Suggest events for my school to earn Fairtrade accreditation'?'

1   Coffee mornings: Host Fairtrade coffee mornings for pupils, parents, and staff. Serve Fairtrade coffee, tea, and snacks while educating attendees about Fairtrade principles.

2   Bake sale: Organise a bake sale featuring Fairtrade ingredients. Encourage pupils and parents to bake using Fairtrade chocolate, sugar, and other products.

3   Fashion show: Hold a fashion show showcasing clothing and accessories made from Fairtrade cotton or other sustainable materials. Highlight the importance of fair wages for garment workers.

4   Fairtrade product stall: Set up a stall during school events selling Fairtrade products such as chocolate, coffee, tea, and handicrafts. This raises awareness and encourages purchases.

5   Workshops: Invite Fairtrade representatives to conduct workshops on Fairtrade principles, its impact on producers, and the significance of ethical consumerism.

6   Art exhibition: Organise an art exhibition featuring pupil artwork related to Fairtrade and ethical trade practices. You can also invite local artists to contribute.

7   Ethical cooking classes: Collaborate with a local chef to provide cooking classes that use Fairtrade ingredients. Pupils can learn how to prepare delicious, ethical meals.

5   See https://schools.fairtrade.org.uk/fairtrade-schools-awards.

8   Awareness week: Dedicate a week to promoting Fairtrade awareness. Plan a series of activities, such as film screenings, guest speakers, and discussions about Fairtrade.

9   Quiz and competitions: Host Fairtrade quizzes and competitions to engage pupils and test their knowledge of Fairtrade principles. Prizes can include Fairtrade products.

10 Educational workshops: Incorporate Fairtrade topics into the curriculum. This can include lessons on the history of Fairtrade, its impact on communities, and the significance of ethical trade.

11 Fundraisers for Fairtrade: Raise funds to support Fairtrade initiatives in developing countries. Consider hosting charity events, fun runs, or other fundraisers.

12 Fairtrade committee: Establish a Fairtrade committee within the school, consisting of teachers, pupils, and parents. This committee can oversee Fairtrade initiatives and promote Fairtrade values within the school.

13 Pledges: Encourage pupils, teachers, and parents to take a Fairtrade pledge, committing to purchase and use Fairtrade products at home and in their daily lives.

14 Participate in Fairtrade Fortnight: Every year, Fairtrade Fortnight is an opportunity to participate in and promote Fairtrade events. Get involved by organising activities during this period.

Remember that achieving Fairtrade accreditation is a process that takes time and dedication. Engage with your local Fairtrade organisation for guidance and support, as they can provide resources and assist in the accreditation process.

Activities suggested by AI could also be used to help schools attain an Eco-Schools Award, LGBT accreditation and so on. For example, it is possible to be awarded an LGBT charter from LGBT Youth Scotland. AI could be used to help update or improve inclusion policies and resources.

65. School Assemblies

You might find yourself entrusted with leading an assembly, an experience that I consider to be immensely valuable for any teacher. It is important to note that you don't necessarily need to be (or aspire to be) in a leadership position to lead a whole-school assembly effectively. This is especially true in an age where AI apps or websites can assist in planning such events. A very basic prompt can generate a high-quality assembly plan.

Prompt: 'Plan a 40-minute whole-school primary assembly on the Harvest Festival and include 10 minutes for "Pupil of the Week Awards".'

Harvest Festival Assembly: Celebrating Nature's Bounty

Duration: 60 minutes

1   Introduction (5 minutes):
  - Welcome everyone and thank them for joining the assembly.
  - Briefly explain the purpose of the assembly: to celebrate the Harvest Festival, a time to appreciate nature's bounty and show gratitude.
  - Share a relevant quote about harvest and gratitude to set the tone.

2   Harvest Festival history and significance (5 minutes):
  - Discuss the origins of the Harvest Festival, its historical and cultural significance.
  - Emphasise the importance of showing gratitude for the food we have and the hard work of farmers.

3   Harvest celebrations around the world (5 minutes):
  - Display a world map and highlight various countries' harvest festivals and traditions.
  - Briefly talk about some unique customs, foods, and activities associated with these celebrations.

4   The importance of giving (5 minutes):
  - Explain how the harvest season also signifies giving back to the community.

- Mention the tradition of donating a portion of the harvest to those in need.
- Share a heart-warming story or example of generosity during the harvest season.

5   Harvest-themed activity (5 minutes):

- Engage pupils in a short interactive activity related to the harvest theme, such as a fun harvest-related quiz or a guessing game about different types of crops.

6   Pupil of the Week Awards (10 minutes):

- Introduce the 'Pupil of the Week' awards segment.
- Call up each awardee and share a brief summary of their accomplishments or positive qualities.
- Present certificates or small prizes to the awardees.
- Encourage applause and cheers from the audience to make the awardees feel special.

7   Harvest crafts display (5 minutes):

- Showcase artwork and crafts created by pupils related to the harvest festival theme.
- Explain the creative process behind some of the crafts and their significance.

8   Gratitude and closing (5 minutes):

- Reiterate the importance of gratitude and appreciation for the blessings we have.
- Invite pupils to take a moment to reflect on something they are thankful for.
- Conclude with a message about coming together as a community to celebrate and support one another.

9   Announcements (5 minutes):

- Make any necessary school announcements regarding upcoming events, activities, or important dates.
- Remind pupils of the collection for donations (e.g. non-perishable food items) for those in need.

10 Closing remarks (5 minutes):

- Thank pupils, teachers, and staff for their participation.
- Encourage everyone to carry the spirit of gratitude and giving beyond the assembly.
- Invite everyone to join in a round of applause for the organisers and participants.

Note: The timings provided are approximate and can be adjusted based on the actual flow of the assembly. Additionally, you can add visuals, videos, or other multimedia elements to enhance engagement. If this sequence is too long for your usual assembly, activities 3, 5 and 7 can be removed.

66. Quizzes

Quizzes serve as excellent whole-class activities. They are beneficial not only for assessment purposes but also highly enjoyable as entertainment, especially in anticipation of upcoming holidays and other special occasions. Quizzes can engage the entire class while also providing an effective measure of pupils' understanding. Furthermore, they offer a platform for interactive learning, enabling pupils to reinforce their knowledge while fostering a sense of friendly competition among peers.

As the Christmas holiday approaches, a fun and light-hearted quiz can create a sense of excitement and anticipation, making this an ideal choice for maintaining engagement and promoting a positive classroom atmosphere. For example, you could ask AI to devise a Christmas movie quiz for you: 'Can you give me 20 quiz questions on well-known children's Christmas movies (with the answers)?'

The Grinch and How the Grinch Stole Christmas:

1   Question: What is the name of the main character who despises Christmas in *How the Grinch Stole Christmas*?

    Answer: The Grinch.

2   Question: In the movie, where does the Grinch live?

    Answer: Mount Crumpit.

3   Question: What is the name of the little girl who befriends the Grinch and helps him understand the true meaning of Christmas?

    Answer: Cindy Lou Who.

Home Alone:

4   Question: In *Home Alone*, what is the name of the main character who gets accidentally left behind during Christmas vacation?

    Answer: Kevin McCallister.

5   Question: How does the main character defend his home from the burglars?

    Answer: He sets up a series of elaborate traps.

6   Question: What do the burglars call themselves in *Home Alone*?

    Answer: The Wet Bandits (Harry and Marv).

The Polar Express:

7 Question: What is the magical mode of transportation that takes children to the North Pole in *The Polar Express*?

Answer: The Polar Express train.

8 Question: What is the first gift that Santa gives to the main character in the movie?

Answer: A sleigh bell.

9 Question: What does the conductor repeatedly punch to make the train go faster in *The Polar Express*?

Answer: The train's magic ticket.

Elf:

10 Question: In *Elf*, what is the name of the main character who was raised by elves at the North Pole?

Answer: Buddy.

11 Question: What is the name of the department store where Buddy works?

Answer: Gimbels.

12 Question: What toy is Buddy afraid of?

Answer: A jack-in-the-box.

A Christmas Carol:

13 Question: Who is the stingy and miserly main character in *A Christmas Carol* who is visited by three ghosts?

Answer: Ebenezer Scrooge.

14 Question: Name the three ghosts that visit the main character in *A Christmas Carol*.

Answer: The Ghost of Christmas Past, the Ghost of Christmas Present, and the Ghost of Christmas Yet to Come (or Future).

15 Question: What is the name of the poor employee who works for the main character and has a disabled son?

Answer: Bob Cratchit.

Rudolph the Red-Nosed Reindeer:

16 Question: What is special about Rudolph in *Rudolph the Red-Nosed Reindeer?*

Answer: He has a shiny red nose that glows.

17 Question: Who is Rudolph's elf friend who wants to be a dentist instead of making toys?

Answer: Hermey.

18 Question: What is the name of the prospector who befriends Rudolph and his friends on their journey?

Answer: Yukon Cornelius.

Frosty the Snowman:

19 Question: In *Frosty the Snowman*, what brings Frosty to life?

Answer: A magical silk hat.

20 Question: What item serves as Frosty's magical hat?

Answer: A magician's top hat.

Feel free to use these questions and answers for your festive quiz!

67. Films to Support Learning

There is nothing quite like a captivating movie to conclude a learning topic or to keep children engaged on challenging days – those special times between Halloween and Guy Fawkes Night when everyone is tired and experiencing a sugar comedown. With AI, it is easy to find films that align with the topics you are teaching – but, remember, it is essential to verify age ratings and appropriateness and notify parents if you plan to show anything not rated 'U'.

For example, 'Suggest children's films for me about the Second World War.'

Here are some children's films that deal with themes related to the Second World War in a sensitive and age-appropriate manner:

1   *The Boy in the Striped Pyjamas* (2008): While this film is more suitable for older children due to its serious subject matter, it provides a unique perspective on friendship and innocence during the Second World War.

1   *War Horse* (2011): The story revolves around a young man named Albert, and his beloved horse named Joey. The film is set against the backdrop of the First World War and explores the bond between Albert and Joey as they are separated by the war.

2   *When Hitler Stole Pink Rabbit* (2019): This film is based on Judith Kerr's semi-autobiographical novel and tells the story of a young Jewish girl and her family fleeing Nazi Germany.

3   *The Book Thief* (2013): While the film is more suitable for tweens and teens, it offers a moving portrayal of a young girl's life in Nazi Germany as she discovers the power of words.

4   *The Lion, the Witch and the Wardrobe* (2005): Though not exclusively focused on the Second World War, this adaptation of C. S. Lewis's classic novel touches on the theme as the four siblings are evacuated to the countryside during the war.

5   *Jojo Rabbit* (2019): A more satirical take suitable for older children, this film portrays the story of a young German boy with an imaginary friend who happens to be a quirky version of Adolf Hitler.

6   *Annie* (1982, 2014): While not about the Second World War, the 2014 adaptation features an orphanage and the historical context of the Great Depression, which could be discussed as part of a broader history lesson.

7   *The Sound of Music* (1965): This classic musical is set in Austria during the late 1930s, highlighting the importance of family, music, and standing up for one's beliefs.

Remember to review these films yourself to ensure they align with your comfort level regarding the portrayal of historical events and their appropriateness for the intended age group. You can also ensure that you are making all the children in school feel represented by asking AI to 'Suggest children's films with a racially diverse cast.'

1   *Moana* (2016): This Disney animated film is set in the Pacific Islands and follows the adventures of Moana as she embarks on a daring journey to save her people.

2   *Coco* (2017): Another Disney-Pixar masterpiece, this film centres around Mexican culture and the celebration of Dia de los Muertos (Day of the Dead).

3   *The Princess and the Frog* (2009): Disney's first African-American princess takes centre stage in this reimagining of the classic fairy tale set in New Orleans.

4   *Akeelah and the Bee* (2006): This inspirational film follows a young African-American girl with a gift for spelling who aspires to compete in the National Spelling Bee.

5   *Spider-Man: Into the Spider-Verse* (2018): An animated superhero film that introduces audiences to various Spider-People from different dimensions, showcasing diversity in a fun and exciting way.

6   *Matilda* (1996): Based on Roald Dahl's novel, this film adaptation features a racially diverse cast and tells the story of a brilliant young girl with extraordinary abilities.

7   *Big Hero 6* (2014): Set in the fictional city of San Fransokyo, this Disney film follows a young robotics prodigy and his diverse group of friends as they become superheroes.

8   *Home* (2015): An animated film that centres around a young girl named Tip and an alien named Oh, focusing on themes of friendship and acceptance.

9   *Finding Nemo* (2003)/*Finding Dory* (2016): These Pixar films feature a diverse cast of underwater characters and explore themes of family and adventure.

10 *The Karate Kid* (2010): This modern remake of the classic film features a diverse cast and highlights the relationship between a young boy and his martial arts mentor.

11 *Zootopia* (2016): In this animated film, a bunny cop teams up with a sly fox to uncover a conspiracy that threatens the harmony of their diverse city.

12 *Wonder* (2017): While not the central theme, this film includes a racially diverse cast and tells the heart-warming story of a boy with facial differences as he enters mainstream school.

These films offer children the opportunity to see characters from various backgrounds and cultures, promoting inclusivity and understanding. Always review the films to ensure they align with your preferences and values.

68. Scripts for School Shows

School shows can be exciting times in primary schools. The anticipation, the families coming to see their children, the pride on parents' and children's faces, watching quiet children come out of their shell and perform confidently to an audience. And with all this positivity comes a lot of hard work. While school shows are undoubtedly worth the effort, have you ever wished you didn't need to write scripts? Now, AI can do it for you!

The prompt, 'Can you write me a script for a Christmas school show with seven characters,' generates:

A Magical Christmas Adventure

Characters:

Emily: Enthusiastic and curious pupil

Alex: Emily's best friend, full of energy

Mrs Thompson: Kind and patient teacher

Father Christmas: Jolly and magical

Elfie: Father Christmas's mischievous elf assistant

Grace: A shy pupil with a big heart

Max: Energetic and adventurous classmate

Scene 1: Classroom

All characters are sitting in a classroom, working on holiday-themed crafts.

Emily: (Excitedly) Hey, Alex! Can you believe it's almost Christmas?

Alex: (Grinning) I know, right? I can't wait for the school holiday show!

Mrs Thompson: (Smiling) Everyone, don't forget to bring your holiday spirit to the stage!

Scene 2: Santa's Workshop

Emily and Alex discover a magical portal that leads to Santa's Workshop.

Emily: (Gazing at the portal) Whoa, what's this?

Alex: Let's check it out, Emily!

They step through the portal and find themselves in Santa's Workshop.

Scene 3: Santa's Workshop

Father Christmas and Elfie are busy preparing gifts.

Father Christmas: (Chuckling) Welcome, young adventurers! You've entered a magical place.

Elfie: (Whispering to the audience) And I'm Elfie, Father Christmas's trusty helper … when I'm not causing mischief!

Scene 4: Learning the True Meaning

Father Christmas explains the importance of kindness and giving.

Father Christmas: Remember, it's not just about the presents. It's about spreading joy and love.

Emily: (Inspired) You're right, Father Christmas. We want to make this holiday special for everyone.

Scene 5: School Show Rehearsal

Back in the classroom, pupils are rehearsing for the holiday show.

Grace: (Nervously) Um, can I be the tree in the play?

Mrs Thompson: Of course, Grace! You'll be the most wonderful tree.

Scene 6: The Big Performance

The school show begins with various acts, including carol singing, dances, and a play.

Max: (As the narrator) Once upon a time in a snowy land …

Emily and Alex: (Playing the lead roles) (Together) We learned the true meaning of Christmas!

Scene 7: The Finale

Father Christmas and Elfie join the festivities.

Father Christmas: (Booming laughter) Ho ho ho! Well done, young ones.

Elfie: (Hugging the pupils) You've brought joy to everyone's hearts!

Mrs Thompson: (Proudly) And that's what makes this the best holiday show ever.

The cast and pupils come together, singing a heart-warming holiday song.

All: (Singing) Joy and laughter, love and cheer, a magical holiday time of year!

The curtain closes as everyone cheers.

Narrator: (Voiceover) And so, a magical Christmas adventure brought the spirit of the season to life!

You could modify the above by asking it to 'Add two characters to the above and write enough for a 20-minute performance.'

You could also ask AI to construct scripts to use as reading activities to get the children engaged in reading. The possibilities are limitless for developing scripts that are personalised and based on characters the children like or topics they enjoy.

69. AI to Bring Fun to the Classroom

As educators, we are aware of the importance of cultivating strong relationships with our pupils. While it is true that positive relationships won't single-handedly resolve all behaviour issues in schools, they do play a role. I have observed that children have a particular fondness for jokes, especially the kind we often refer to as 'teacher jokes' (i.e. bad jokes). On occasion, I make a promise, or perhaps a playful threat, to share my most recent joke with pupils once they have completed their task. Initially, they grumble, already anticipating a groan-worthy punchline, yet by the end of the lesson, they are eager to hear it!

AI can provide an endless supply of classroom-themed jokes, which, despite being loved and loathed in equal measure, can inject a dose of amusement and merriment into the learning environment.

Prompt: 'Tell me five child-friendly jokes about teachers.'

1 Why did the teacher go to the beach? To test the waters!

2 Why did the maths book look sad? Because it had too many problems!

3 Why did the teacher bring a ladder to school? Because she heard the class was going to a higher level!

4 Why did the teacher wear sunglasses to school? Because her pupils were so bright!

5 What is a teacher's favourite type of music? Class-ical music!

Another creative way to use jokes is to incorporate them into an interactive advent calendar activity. Here are 10 Christmas-themed jokes to bring some holiday cheer:

1 Why was the Christmas tree so bad at knitting? Because it kept dropping its needles!

2 What do you get if you cross a snowman and a vampire? Frostbite!

3 What do elves post on social media? Elf-ies!

4 What do you call a snowman with a sunburn? A puddle!

5 What do you get when you cross a snowman and a dog? Frostbite!

6 Why was the maths book sad during the holidays? It had too many problems!

7 What did one ornament say to the other ornament? 'I like hanging out with you!'

8 What do you call a snowman party? A snowball!

9 What do you call a snowman with a six-pack? An abdominal snowman!

10 Why did the gingerbread cookie go to the doctor? Because it was feeling crumby!

I hope these jokes add some festive laughter to your holiday celebrations!

70. Riddles and Brainteasers

I have had numerous pupils in the past who thoroughly enjoyed attempting to solve riddles. While riddles create some fun and healthy competition, they also possess educational merit. Riddles encourage children to think critically and analytically; they necessitate the analysis of clues, the consideration of diverse perspectives, and logical reasoning; and they also require memory recall and nurture creative thinking and problem-solving skills to find the solution.

By leveraging AI, you can effortlessly generate riddles suitable for children to tackle. You might even consider displaying some of these AI-generated riddles as fast-finisher activities.

1 I have keys but open no locks. I have space but no room. You can enter, but you can't go outside. What am I?

   Answer: A keyboard!

2 What has keys but can't open locks, and comes in all shapes and sizes?

   Answer: A piano!

3 I speak without a mouth and hear without ears. I have no body, but I come alive with the wind. What am I?

   Answer: An echo!

4 I'm full of holes, yet I can hold water. What am I?

   Answer: A sponge!

It is also easy to make riddles seasonal or themed to suit children's interests or learning – for example, 'Tell me some child-friendly space-themed riddles.'

1 I'm a big ball of gas up in the sky, and my fiery light makes night not so shy. What am I?

   Answer: The Sun!

2 I'm round like a pizza, but I'm not something to eat. I have craters and rocks, and astronauts think I'm neat. What am I?

   Answer: The moon!

3 I have eight legs, but I'm not a bug you'd see. I'm known for my rings; some call me 'Lord of the Sea'. What am I?

Answer: Saturn!

4 I'm a red planet, often called the fourth from the sun. Some think I might have had water and life; exploring me sounds like fun. What am I?

Answer: Mars!

5 I'm a huge group of stars, shining oh so bright, forming shapes that people see, like a bear or hunter in the night. What am I?

Answer: A constellation!

6 I'm a fast-moving streak of light, making a wish is what people might do. I'm often seen in the night sky, and I'm sometimes called a 'shooting' one. What am I?

Answer: A shooting star (or meteor)!

7 I'm not a planet, but I'm not a star. I'm a frozen ball that comes from afar. I have a glowing tail when I get near the sun. What am I?

Answer: A comet!

8 I'm a group of planets that circle a star, and Earth is one of us, not too near and not too far. What am I?

Answer: A solar system!

71. Games to Bring Calm

We all have our go-to games and routines to help settle a class, especially after a rainy break when the children have had to stay indoors. However, there are times when these methods lose their effectiveness or the children begin to get bored of them. This is where AI can step in to provide you with fresh ideas for games and strategies to try out.

Prompt: 'Give me suggestions of games to play to help calm a primary class.'

Here are some calming and mindfulness-focused games that you can play with a primary class to help them relax and refocus:

1 Mindful breathing: Guide the pupils through a simple breathing exercise. Have them close their eyes and take slow, deep breaths in and out. You can count the breaths to help them focus.

2 Silent nature walk: If possible, take the class outside for a silent nature walk. Encourage them to pay attention to the sounds, sights, and sensations around them. After the walk, gather to discuss what they observed.

3 Rain stick meditation: Provide each pupil with a rain stick or a small container with rice inside. Instruct them to slowly tilt it back and forth, focusing on the calming sound it makes. This activity helps them to practise mindfulness.

4 Guided visualisation: Lead the pupils through a guided visualisation. Describe a peaceful scene, such as lying on a beach or floating on a cloud. Encourage them to use their imagination to create a mental image.

5 Yoga for children: Introduce simple yoga poses that are suitable for children. Incorporate calming poses like 'child's pose', 'tree pose', and 'butterfly pose'. This helps pupils to stretch, focus on their breathing, and relax their bodies.

6 Mindful colouring: Provide colouring sheets or mandalas for pupils to colour. Encourage them to focus on the sensation of colouring and to choose colours that reflect their feelings.

7 Breathing buddies: Give each pupil a small stuffed animal or toy. Have them lie down with the toy on their stomachs. As they breathe in and out, they can watch the toy rise and fall with their breath.

8 Five senses exercise: Guide pupils to use their five senses to become aware of their surroundings. Ask them to identify five things they can see, four things they can touch, three things they can hear, two things they can smell, and one thing they can taste (if appropriate).

9 Quiet corner: Designate a cosy corner of the classroom as a 'quiet corner'. Stock it with soft cushions or bean bags and some calming activities like books, soft toys, or sensory items. Pupils can use this space whenever they need a moment to calm down.

10 Storytelling meditation: Share a short, calming story with the class, focusing on peaceful settings and positive outcomes. Afterwards, ask pupils to share their thoughts and feelings about the story.

Remember that consistency is key when introducing calming activities to a primary class. Over time, these activities can become part of the classroom routine, helping pupils to develop self-regulation skills and cope with stress or restlessness.

72. Noisy Classrooms

Noise can be useful and productive for some learning tasks, but there are times when focus and concentration is required. So, what about those classes who only have two volumes – loud and louder? AI can give you a list of strategies to try for those times when you want the children to be silent.

Prompt: 'Can you give me strategies to promote quiet concentration in a young primary class?'

Certainly! Promoting quiet concentration in a young primary class requires a combination of structured routines, engaging activities, and techniques that help children to develop self-regulation skills. Here are some strategies to consider:

1   Establish clear expectations: Set clear guidelines for when quiet concentration is expected, such as during independent work or quiet reading time. Explain to the pupils why quiet concentration is important and how it helps them learn.

2   Design a calm workspace: Create a designated area in the classroom where pupils can work quietly. Arrange desks or cushions in a way that minimises distractions and provides a sense of personal space.

3   Use soft lighting: Opt for soft and natural lighting to create a calming atmosphere. Harsh or bright lighting can lead to restlessness in some children.

4   Mindful transitions: Teach pupils to transition quietly from one activity to another. Use a chime or a calming sound to signal transitions, encouraging them to listen attentively and transition without disruption.

5   Quiet signals: Establish quiet signals that you use consistently, such as raising your hand or using a visual cue. When pupils see the signal, they know it is time to focus and work quietly.

6   Breathing breaks: Introduce short breathing breaks throughout the day. Teach pupils simple breathing exercises they can use to calm themselves and refocus.

7   Guided visualisation: Guide pupils through brief guided visualisations to help them relax and concentrate. For example, ask them to imagine a peaceful place or picture themselves successfully completing a task.

8   Soft background music: Play soft instrumental music in the background during quiet activities. Music can help to create a calming environment and drown out potential distractions.

9   Noise-cancelling headphones: Provide noise-cancelling headphones for pupils who are particularly sensitive to auditory distractions. This can help them to concentrate better on their tasks.

10 Mindful activities: Introduce mindfulness activities, such as colouring, simple yoga poses, or mindful breathing exercises, to help pupils practise concentration and self-awareness.

11 Use timers: Set a timer for specific periods of quiet concentration. This can create a sense of urgency and help children to stay focused on their tasks.

12 Model quiet concentration: Model the behaviour you want to see. When pupils observe you engaged in quiet work, they are more likely to follow suit.

13 Positive reinforcement: Praise and reward pupils when they exhibit quiet concentration. Positive reinforcement can motivate them to continue the behaviour.

14 Progressive relaxation: Teach pupils progressive muscle relaxation techniques. This involves tensing and then relaxing different muscle groups, helping them to release tension and stay focused.

15 Transition to independent work gradually: When transitioning from a lively activity to quiet work, do it gradually. Use calming activities, such as reading a story or doing a quiet game, to ease them into a focused mindset.

Remember that young children have varying attention spans, so it is important to gradually build their capacity for quiet concentration over time. Implementing a combination of these strategies and tailoring them to your pupils' needs will help to create a classroom environment conducive to calm focus and learning.

73. Simple Time Filler Games

In the primary environment, it is crucial to eliminate any 'dead time', as children can become bored and chaos may ensue. It is vital to have some effective classroom management strategies, like simple and engaging games, for intermediate moments – for example, when the children are waiting for activities such as break or assembly or when unforeseen delays occur.

If the time comes and you don't have any games prepared, you can quickly access them through an AI app on your phone. You could even introduce the game by saying, 'Who would like to try out this new game? Let me explain the rules ...'

Prompt: 'Tell me some simple classroom time-filler games for children.'

1 20 Questions: Choose an object in the classroom, and have the children take turns asking 'yes' or 'no' questions to guess what it is. They have 20 questions to figure it out.

2 I Spy: Select an object in the room and say, 'I spy with my little eye, something that is ...' followed by a clue (colour, shape, location). Children take turns guessing the object.

3 Simon Says: You give commands but the children should only follow if you say 'Simon says' before the command. For example, 'Simon says touch your nose.'

4 Alphabet Categories: Choose a category (animals, foods, etc.) and take turns naming items from that category in alphabetical order. For instance, 'A is for apple, B is for banana ...'

5 Word Chain: Start with a word and have the children take turns saying words that start with the last letter of the previous word. For example, 'cat', 'tree', 'elephant'.

6 Memory Game: Place a few objects on a tray and let the children look at them for a minute. Then cover the tray and remove one object. The children have to guess which object is missing.

7 Charades: Write simple words on cards (actions, animals, objects) and have the children take turns acting out the word without speaking while others guess what it is.

8 Pictionary: Similar to charades, but the child draws the word on the board while others guess what it is.

9 Quiet Ball: Children sit in a circle. Toss a soft ball to one child and ask them a question. They answer and then toss the ball to another child to ask a new question.

10 Counting Claps: Start by clapping once, then the next child claps twice, the next child claps three times, and so on. See how high you can count together.

11 Paper Plate Frisbees: Give each child a paper plate and have them decorate it with markers. Then have a mini 'frisbee' throwing contest.

12 Name That Tune: Play a few seconds of a familiar song and have the children guess the title.

13 Bubble Wrap Stomp: Place a sheet of bubble wrap on the floor. Let the children take turns stomping on it to hear the satisfying pops.

14 Story Starters: Begin a story with a sentence and have the children take turns adding a sentence to build the story together.

These games are not only enjoyable but also help in building various skills such as communication, teamwork, creativity, and focus. They can be great tools to have on hand when you need a quick activity to fill a short gap of time in the classroom.

74. Planning for After-School Clubs

Many teachers enjoy participating in after-school clubs, which can bring numerous benefits to the school community. However, despite our best intentions, our schedules are often so packed that dedicating even an hour to a club during the week can feel like a drain on our resources. Thankfully, AI can not only alleviate the burden of routine lesson planning but also extend its utility to organising after-school clubs.

Let's explore this idea further with the example of an after-school drama club. Prompt: 'Can you plan a six-week block of drama club sessions for 7-year-olds?'

Week 1 – introduction to drama:

- Objective: Introduce children to the concept of drama and build a comfortable environment for expression.
- Icebreaker activity: 'Name in Motion' – each child says their name with a movement. The group imitates the movement and says the child's name in unison.
- Group circle: Discuss what drama is by asking questions like 'What is your favourite thing about pretending?' and 'Why do you like to use your imagination?'
- Imaginary play: 'Animal Kingdom' – children take turns choosing an animal and then everyone in the group moves and sounds like that animal.
- Story starters: Each child takes a turn completing the sentence, 'In my favourite place, I like to …'

Week 2 – expressive movement:

- Objective: Develop body awareness and expression through movement.
- Warm-up: 'Mirror, Mirror' – children work in pairs. One child leads the movements while the other imitates as if they are looking in a mirror. Switch roles.
- Freeze dance: Play energetic music and pause it suddenly. Children freeze in creative poses. Repeat with different styles of music.
- Character parade: Each child chooses a character (real or imaginary) and parades around the room, moving and acting like that character.

Week 3 – storytelling:

- Objective: Introduce the basics of storytelling and character development.

- Warm-up: 'Zip, Zap, Zop' – children stand in a circle. One child says 'zip', the next says 'zap', and the next says 'zop'. The pattern continues. If a child says 'zap' while making eye contact with another, that child must say 'zip' to reverse the direction.[6]

- Group story: Children sit in a circle. Begin a story with a sentence, then go around the circle, with each child adding a sentence to build the story.

- Creating characters: Each child chooses a prop from a box (hat, scarf, toy) and creates a short skit where they are a character who uses that prop.

Week 4 – improvisation:

- Objective: Encourage quick thinking and creative responses.

- Warm-up: 'Word Association' – children stand in a circle. One child says a word, the next child says a word related to the first, and so on.

- Freeze improv: Children move around the space. When the leader calls out a situation ('You're on a pirate ship!'), children freeze and then act out that scenario.

- Improv pairs: Children work in pairs. One child starts a sentence with 'I think we're lost in the jungle,' and the other child responds with an improvised line. They take turns continuing the conversation.

Week 5 – mini performances:

- Objective: Develop confidence through small group performances.

- Warm-up: 'Copycat Charades' – children take turns acting out simple words while others guess.

- Mini performances: Divide children into small groups. Each group receives a prop and must create a short skit that includes the prop, a specific location (beach, space, jungle), and characters of their choice. They can use the skills they have learned in previous weeks.

Week 6 – creative play:

- Objective: Encourage children to collaborate and think creatively.

---

6   Only zip changes the direction. If someone hesitates, says the wrong word or breaks the rhythm, they are out for that round. Hand actions such as a clap can be added to the words for variation.

- Warm-up: 'Statues' – play music. When the music stops, children freeze in a pose. Encourage imaginative and dynamic poses.

- Collaborative skits: Divide the children into groups. Each group receives a prop, a location, and characters. They collaboratively create a skit that incorporates all elements. After each group performs, have a short discussion about what they enjoyed most.

Feel free to adapt these plans based on the interests and energy level of the children. The main goal is to foster their creativity, build their confidence, and have fun exploring the world of drama!

75. Emotional Literacy

Emotional literacy – the ability to express emotions and feelings using speech and other forms of communication – is becoming increasingly important in the contemporary classroom. Many AI platforms have image generators that can assist teachers in creating lessons that young children will understand. For example, a simple request for a 'sad face' will quickly yield an image that can be used as a stimulus for class discussion. You could ask the children to explore, 'How do we recognise another person's sadness?' or 'What does sadness feel like?' This could be reversed by first having the discussion and then showing the image to the children.

During well-being check-ins, pupils often default to saying that they are either 'happy' or 'sad'. AI can support the development of children's self-awareness and emotional intelligence by facilitating discussion on a wider range of emotions and giving them concrete examples of the nuances involved in these emotions. Furthermore, AI can provide a detailed lesson plan.

Prompt: 'Plan an emotional literacy lesson for children using AI generated images of emotions.'

Exploring Emotions Through AI-Generated Images

Duration: 60 minutes

Objective:

- To help pupils understand and identify different emotions.
- To improve emotional literacy and empathy skills.

Materials:

- AI-generated images of emotions (happy, sad, angry, surprised, and confused)
- Whiteboard or chalkboard and markers/chalk
- Projector and screen
- Paper and coloured pencils/crayons/markers
- Emotion flashcards (optional)
- Internet access (for displaying AI-generated images)

Lesson plan:

1 Introduction (10 minutes):

- Begin by discussing the importance of emotions and how they play a significant role in our daily lives. Emphasise that emotions can affect how we feel, think, and interact with others.

- Introduce the concept of emotional literacy, explaining that it is the ability to recognise and understand our emotions and the emotions of others. Share that today's lesson will focus on improving their emotional literacy skills.

2 Emotion identification activity (15 minutes):

- Display AI-generated images of emotions one by one on the screen. Ask pupils to observe each image and guess the emotion it represents.

- After each image, have a brief class discussion where pupils share their thoughts on what they saw and why they think it represents a particular emotion.

- Keep a list on the whiteboard/chalkboard of the emotions identified, and make sure to discuss why certain facial expressions or body language convey those emotions.

3 Emotion charades activity (15 minutes):

- Divide the class into small groups of three or four pupils.

- Provide each group with a set of emotion flashcards or written emotion prompts (e.g. 'happy', 'angry', 'surprised').

- In each group, one pupil will draw an emotion card and act out the emotion without speaking, while the others try to guess the emotion being portrayed.

- Rotate roles within each group, so every pupil has a chance to act out an emotion.

- After each round, encourage a brief discussion about the challenges and experiences each group had in recognising and portraying emotions.

4 Create your emotion artwork activity (15 minutes):

- Distribute paper and art supplies (coloured pencils, crayons, markers) to the pupils.

- Instruct them to choose one emotion from the list discussed earlier or one they find particularly interesting. Have them draw a picture that represents this emotion.
- Encourage pupils to be creative and use colours, shapes, and expressions to convey the chosen emotion.

5 Conclusion (5 minutes):

- Ask each pupil to share their emotion artwork with the class, explaining why they chose that emotion and how they represented it.
- Reinforce the idea that understanding and expressing emotions is an essential skill for building strong relationships and empathy.
- Discuss the role of AI in generating images and how technology can assist us in understanding emotions.
- Assign a brief homework task where pupils are encouraged to notice and record instances of different emotions in their daily lives, either through drawings, descriptions, or photos.

Assessment (optional):

- You can assess pupils' understanding of emotions and emotional literacy by reviewing their artwork and the insights they share during class discussions. Additionally, you can assign a short reflection essay or journal entry where pupils discuss what they learned about emotions and how it applies to their lives.

76. Mindfulness in the Classroom

Many behaviour issues in schools have become more pronounced since the COVID-19 lockdowns. Teachers are reporting a decrease in social skills and higher levels of violence among pupils. In addition, many more children and young people are suffering from poor mental health. There is no silver bullet for these problems, and teachers cannot compensate for mental health services that are stretched to the limit. However, there is great merit in using relaxation techniques and mindfulness in the classroom to foster pupil (and staff) well-being.

If you are interested in introducing mindfulness games and activities to help the children relax and focus, AI can provide some helpful suggestions. Here are five mindfulness games that can be used with children in school.

1 Mindful listening:
- Instruct the children to sit quietly and close their eyes.
- Ask them to focus on the sounds around them, both near and far.
- After a few minutes, have them share the different sounds they heard.

2 Mindful breathing:
- Guide the children to sit comfortably with their eyes closed.
- Ask them to take slow, deep breaths in through their nose and out through their mouth.
- Encourage them to focus on the sensation of their breath entering and leaving their body.
- Repeat this for a few minutes, reminding them to bring their attention back to their breath whenever their mind wanders.

3 Mindful observation:
- Provide each child with a small object, such as a pebble or a leaf.
- Instruct them to hold the object in their hands and observe it closely.
- Encourage them to notice the colour, texture, shape, and any other details of the object.
- After a few minutes, have them share their observations with the class.

4 Mindful movement:

- Lead the children in a series of slow and deliberate movements, such as stretching, reaching, and bending.
- Encourage them to pay attention to the sensations in their body as they move.
- Remind them to focus on their breath and stay present in the moment.

5 Mindful gratitude:

- Have the children sit in a circle and take turns sharing something they are grateful for.
- Encourage them to be specific and explain why they are grateful for that particular thing or person.
- Remind them to listen attentively to their classmates' expressions of gratitude.

These mindfulness games can help the children to develop focus, self-awareness, and emotional regulation. They can be incorporated into the daily routine or used as a break during the school day to promote calmness and well-being.

In addition to my role as a primary teacher, I am also a certified yoga instructor with a specialisation in children's yoga, meditation, and mindfulness. From this perspective, I find the activities recommended by the AI app to be highly beneficial. However, it is important to consider the context and individual dynamics of your classroom. Understanding your pupils and being attuned to situations when certain activities, such as focusing on gratitude, might not be suitable for a particular child is crucial. However, as educators, we are skilled at making these professional judgements every day.

77. Meditation

Some people find meditation challenging because they overthink it and worry about 'doing it right'. Guided meditations circumvent this problem, enabling children to simply listen and relax. AI can be employed to craft beautiful guided meditations suitable for classroom use. These meditations could encompass seasonal themes, connect with the curriculum, or focus purely on improving children's well-being and relaxation. Meditation has also been shown to improve concentration – an educational bonus. Furthermore, guided or narrative-based meditations introduce pupils to intricate language patterns and therefore expand their vocabulary too.

Prompt: 'Write me an autumn-day-themed meditation for children.'

Enchanted Autumn Journey

Welcome, children, to a magical journey through the golden embrace of autumn. Find a comfortable spot to sit or lie down, allowing your body to settle and your mind to relax. Close your eyes and take a deep, calming breath in through your nose and slowly exhale through your mouth.

Imagine you are standing at the edge of a mystical forest. The trees around you are adorned with leaves of brilliant oranges, fiery reds, and warm yellows. The air is crisp, carrying the gentle scent of fallen leaves and earth.

As you step into the forest, the leaves crunch beneath your feet, creating a soothing melody. The sunlight filters through the canopy above, casting dappled patterns of light and shadow on the ground. Feel the gentle warmth of the sun on your skin and the cool, refreshing breeze on your face.

Ahead, you spot a narrow path paved with the softest carpet of leaves. Follow this path deeper into the heart of the forest. Along the way, you come across a friendly squirrel gathering acorns and a curious rabbit peeking out from behind a tree.

As you continue on your journey, you stumble upon a cosy clearing. In the centre of this clearing, there is a bubbling brook with crystal-clear water. The sunlight dances on the water's surface, creating a mesmerising display of shimmering reflections.

Sit by the brook and dip your fingers into the water. Feel its coolness and purity as it flows over your skin. Imagine that with each touch of the water, any worries or tension within you are gently washed away, leaving you feeling light and peaceful.

Now, let's take a moment to listen to the sounds of the forest. Close your eyes and let the rustling leaves, chirping birds, and gentle whispers of the wind fill your ears. Allow these soothing sounds to envelop you in a comforting embrace.

As you bask in the tranquillity of this enchanted forest, take a deep breath in, drawing in the energy and beauty of the autumn season. Exhale slowly, releasing any lingering stress or worries.

When you are ready, slowly open your eyes and bring your awareness back to the present moment. Carry the serenity of this autumn journey with you, knowing that you can return to this magical place in your imagination whenever you need a moment of calm.

Remember, just like the leaves that gracefully fall from the trees, you too can let go of anything that no longer serves you, making space for new and wonderful experiences in your life.

Take one last deep breath in, and as you exhale, gently wiggle your fingers and toes, bringing yourself back fully.

78. Supporting Positive Friendships

Surprisingly, AI can be useful in planning lessons that teach children how to navigate their friendships and difficult social situations. We have all had older classes where the children are starting to develop their personalities and sense of self, which can sometimes result in friction and friendship issues.

Prompt: 'Can you plan a lesson to help children resolve a fall-out among friends?'

Resolving Friendship Conflicts

Objective: To teach children conflict resolution strategies to help them manage and resolve disagreements with friends in a respectful and empathetic manner.

Grade level: Ages 7–11

Duration: Approximately 45–60 minutes

Materials:

- Whiteboard or chalkboard
- Markers or chalk
- Construction paper
- Scissors
- Glue
- Handout with conflict resolution steps (optional)

Lesson steps:

1 Introduction (10 minutes):

- Begin with a brief discussion about friendships and how conflicts can sometimes arise among friends.
- Ask open-ended questions to encourage children to share their experiences with conflicts and how they feel when disagreements occur.

2   Brainstorming conflict scenarios (10 minutes):

- On the whiteboard, list several conflict scenarios relevant to children's lives, such as sharing toys, disagreeing about a game, or misunderstanding a comment.

- Ask pupils to choose one scenario and think about how they would feel and react if they were involved in that situation.

3   Small group discussions (15 minutes):

- Divide the class into small groups of four or five pupils.

- Assign each group a scenario to discuss. Encourage them to share their thoughts, feelings, and possible solutions for resolving the conflict.

- Have a group spokesperson share their discussion outcomes with the whole class.

4   Conflict resolution strategies (10 minutes):

- Discuss common conflict resolution strategies, such as:

  - Talking calmly and listening to each other.

  - Expressing feelings using 'I' statements (e.g. 'I felt hurt when …').

  - Finding compromises that make both parties happy.

  - Apologising and forgiving.

- Emphasise the importance of using respectful language and considering each other's feelings.

5   Friendship flowers craft activity (10 minutes):

- Provide each pupil with construction paper, scissors, and glue.

- Instruct pupils to create a flower with several petals. On each petal, they can write a conflict resolution strategy they have learned.

- Once the petals are ready, have pupils glue them around a centre circle to form a 'friendship flower'.

6   Role-playing (5 minutes):

- Engage the pupils in a brief role-playing activity. Pair them up and have them act out a conflict scenario using the strategies they have learned.

7   Wrap-up and reflection (5 minutes):

- Gather the class and ask pupils to share one thing they have learned about resolving conflicts among friends.

- Emphasise that disagreements are a normal part of friendships and that using these strategies can help to maintain healthy relationships.

Extension activities:

- Have pupils create posters illustrating the conflict resolution steps and display them in the classroom.

- Encourage pupils to share their newfound conflict resolution skills with their friends and family.

Assessment:

- Monitor class discussions and small group interactions to ensure pupils are actively engaged and sharing their ideas.

- Evaluate the pupils' craft activity and role-playing to gauge their understanding of conflict resolution strategies.

By guiding pupils through these conflict resolution strategies, you are not only helping them to address current issues but also equipping them with valuable skills that will serve them well in their relationships throughout life.

79. School Policies for Pupils

AI is excellent at creating school policies. For example, the debate surrounding mobile phones in schools is substantial. Whether you currently hold a leadership role or aspire to do so, you might find yourself responsible for formulating a mobile phone policy. If you have devised a preliminary outline of the policy, AI can assist in completing the details, thereby streamlining the process and saving you time.

It is possible to type an unsophisticated word salad into an AI app – for example, 'Create a school pupil mobile phone policy saying we support pupils having mobile phones for safety travelling to and from school but require them to be handed into the office for pupil and cyber safety during the school day,' and it will generate a coherent policy.

School Pupil Mobile Phone Policy

At [School Name], we recognise the importance of ensuring our pupils' safety while travelling to and from school. We also acknowledge the role that mobile phones play in today's world. As such, we have developed the following mobile phone policy to strike a balance between pupil safety and maintaining an effective learning environment.

1   Mobile phones for travel safety:

We understand that many pupils use mobile phones as a means of communication and safety while travelling to and from school. Pupils are encouraged to have their mobile phones with them during their commute for emergency purposes.

2   Mobile phone usage during school hours:

To maintain a focused and secure learning environment, we require all pupils to hand in their mobile phones at the school office upon arrival. This policy is designed to safeguard pupils' well-being, both physically and in the digital realm.

3   Reasons for mobile phone submission:

   a   Pupil safety: Handing in mobile phones prevents distractions during class and minimises the risk of theft, loss, or damage during school hours.

   b   Cyber safety: We aim to ensure a safe online environment for all pupils. By restricting mobile phone use during school hours, we reduce the potential for cyberbullying, inappropriate content sharing, or other online safety concerns.

c   Academic focus: Deterring mobile phone use during class helps pupils to concentrate on their studies and engage in meaningful learning activities.

4   Mobile phone storage:

Mobile phones submitted to the office will be securely stored until the end of the school day. Pupils can retrieve their phones when classes conclude.

5   Exceptions:

In special circumstances, such as school projects, teacher-approved activities, or emergencies, pupils may use their mobile phones under the guidance of a teacher.

6   Consequences of violation:

Any violation of the mobile phone policy will be addressed in accordance with the school's disciplinary procedures. This may include warnings, confiscation, or parental involvement, depending on the severity and frequency of the violation.

7   Communication:

We encourage parents and guardians to communicate with the school office for any specific concerns or arrangements regarding their child's mobile phone usage.

By adhering to this mobile phone policy, we are committed to fostering a secure, respectful, and productive educational environment for all pupils at [School Name].

This policy is effective from [Effective Date] and is subject to periodic review to ensure its relevance and effectiveness in maintaining a positive school experience for our pupils.

80. Creating Meaningful Visual Timetables

While many of us have access to resources for creating visual timetables, AI presents an exciting opportunity to personalise these tools even further, tailoring them to the unique needs of each child. Visual timetables are important for many children but particularly children who are autistic and need the predictability and reassurance that comes from a graphic reminder of the activities happening throughout the day. With AI, and particularly with text-to-image generators, you can make these timetables much more customised and relevant to the individual child.

For instance, a child who enjoys eating crisps might benefit from some visuals that truly reflect their snacking preferences. This might include an image of a child resembling them who is eating a red bag of their favourite ready-salted crisps! Likewise, a child who lives in a high-rise apartment might resonate more with an accurate representation of their home rather than a generic image of a cookie-cutter house, thereby elevating the relevance of the timetable for that child.

AI can also minimise the barriers for children with learning disabilities by displaying timetabled information in pictorial ways that are easier for them to interpret.

81. Ensuring an Inclusive and Decolonised Curriculum

Many educators are currently taking steps towards implementing a decolonised curriculum. Manchester Metropolitan University defines decolonising the curriculum as the process of 'identifying, acknowledging and challenging the ways in which colonialism has impacted upon perceived knowledge and learning'.[7]

Achieving this goal is more straightforward than it might seem initially. For example, it could involve discussing the contributions of the Arab world to mathematics or ensuring that the narratives we teach about the Second World War are not centred exclusively around white Europeans. Some educators may lack confidence in their ability to undertake this task, but AI can greatly simplify the process.

For example, simply type into an AI app, 'Can you tell me some racially diverse Second World War history?'

The Second World War was a global conflict involving a wide range of countries and people from different racial and ethnic backgrounds. Here are some examples of racial diversity in Second World War history:

1 Tuskegee Airmen: The Tuskegee Airmen were a group of African-American pilots, navigators, and support personnel who served in the United States Army Air Forces during the Second World War. They faced racial discrimination and scepticism about their abilities, but they proved their excellence as fighter pilots and played a significant role in the air war over Europe.

2 Navajo Code Talkers: Native Americans from the Navajo Nation served as code talkers in the Pacific theatre. They used their native language to create an unbreakable code that the Japanese couldn't decipher, providing secure communication for the US military.

3 Japanese Americans: Despite facing discrimination and being placed in internment camps on American soil, many Japanese Americans also served in the US military. The 442nd Regimental Combat Team, composed primarily of Japanese Americans, became one of the most decorated units in US military history.

7 See https://www.mmu.ac.uk/about-us/professional-services/uta/reducing-awarding-gaps/decolonising-the-curriculum-toolkit.

4   British Indian Army: Millions of soldiers from the Indian subcontinent fought for the British Empire during the Second World War. The British Indian Army included soldiers from various religious and ethnic backgrounds, and they fought in various theatres of the war, such as North Africa, Europe, and Southeast Asia.

5   Chinese Resistance: China was one of the major fronts in the Pacific theatre, and Chinese resistance against Japanese aggression was crucial. The Chinese forces, often facing overwhelming odds, played a significant role in tying down Japanese forces and preventing them from focusing entirely on other fronts.

6   Soviet Red Army: The Soviet Union, a multi-ethnic nation, contributed immensely to the defeat of Nazi Germany. Soldiers and officers from various ethnic backgrounds fought together in the Red Army, with many displaying great bravery and sacrifice.

7   French Colonial Troops: France and its colonies also played a role in the Second World War. Soldiers from various French colonies in Africa and Asia were involved in the conflict, and their contributions often go overlooked.

8   Australian and New Zealand Army Corps (ANZAC): The ANZAC forces consisted of soldiers from diverse backgrounds. These forces played crucial roles in various campaigns, including the battles in Europe, North Africa, and the Pacific.

9   Sikh Soldiers: Sikh soldiers from India served in various Allied forces, including the British Army. Their distinctive appearance, with turbans and beards, made them stand out, but they were known for their bravery and resilience in battle.

10   Ethiopian Resistance: When Italy invaded Ethiopia, Emperor Haile Selassie went into exile but continued to rally support against the occupation. Ethiopian resistance forces, alongside British and Commonwealth troops, eventually helped liberate their country.

These are just a few examples of the racial diversity present in Second World War history. The contributions and sacrifices of people from various racial and ethnic backgrounds played a significant role in shaping the outcome of the war.

This list gives you a place to start. You may wish to begin with the British Indian Army and use AI to find out more information about this fighting force or to plan a lesson. You could also ask AI to tell you about the discrimination of gay and lesbian soldiers during the Second World War; it will produce lots of prompts.

It is worth noting that, when it comes to history, AI apps tend to default to Western, heteronormative, and male-centred narratives. It is important, therefore, to remember about inclusivity – which, as we have seen, it can do when asked.

82. Outdoor Learning Anywhere

Outdoor learning is a crucial element in primary and early education. In an ideal scenario, we would all have access to woodlands and beaches, enabling us to engage in the diverse array of outdoor learning activities showcased on platforms like Pinterest. However, the unfortunate reality is that, for many of us, the playground resembles more of a concrete jungle. As an enthusiast of outdoor learning who experiences the limitations of lacking a personal woodland, I was excited to discover that AI can offer a plethora of suggested learning activities suitable for any environment.

Prompt: 'Suggest outdoor learning activities for children I can do in a concrete playground.'

1 Nature scavenger hunt: Even in a concrete playground, you can hide small natural objects like leaves, pebbles, or flowers. Give children a list of items to find, encouraging observation skills.

2 Pavement chalk art: Use colourful chalk to create art and educational games like hopscotch, number lines, or spelling words.

3 Shadow tracing: Have children trace the shadows of various objects at different times of the day. Discuss how the position of the sun affects the length and direction of shadows.

4 Maths in action: Use the playground's lines, shapes, and measurements to teach maths concepts. Have children estimate distances, count steps, or explore symmetry.

5 Story stones: Paint or draw pictures on stones to represent characters, objects, or scenes from stories. Encourage children to use the stones to create their own imaginative stories.

6 Sensory exploration: Set up sensory stations with materials like sand, water, leaves, and smooth rocks. Children can explore textures, make patterns, and describe their findings.

7 Plant observation: Even in pots or small spaces, you can plant seeds or small plants. Have children document growth and changes over time.

8 Mathematical patterns: Use objects like cones, sticks, or even skipping ropes to create patterns on the ground. Children can extend the patterns or create their own.

9   Outdoor science experiments: Conduct simple science experiments like observing how water evaporates on a sunny day or how objects cast shadows.

10 Nature art: Collect fallen leaves, petals, or twigs to create art pieces. You can make leaf rubbings, create collages, or design temporary installations.

11 Outdoor reading corner: Create a cosy reading corner with cushions and blankets. Children can enjoy books related to nature or any topic you are studying.

12 Map exploration: Draw a map of the playground and mark different areas with symbols. Use this map to guide children on exploration journeys.

13 Alphabet hunt: Have children search for objects in the playground that begin with each letter of the alphabet.

14 Obstacle course: Design a fun and educational obstacle course that incorporates physical activity with learning challenges like solving maths problems or answering trivia questions.

15 Weather observations: Record daily weather conditions and changes in the sky. Discuss patterns and how weather affects the environment.

Remember to adapt these activities to the age and abilities of the children and encourage their curiosity and creativity as they explore and learn in the concrete playground.

83. AI for Overcoming Period Barriers and Reducing Stigma

Ensuring inclusivity within schools is a shared commitment among educators. It is important to acknowledge that many primary-aged children begin experiencing menstruation, underscoring the importance of providing them with adequate support, access to necessary products, and assistance in managing period pain.

Regrettably, not all schools are equipped with a dedicated nurse's office where pupils experiencing menstrual pain can find respite. Nonetheless, as always, we strive to optimise the resources at our disposal to address these needs to the best of our abilities.

AI can offer useful guidance in this realm and aid in the formulation of compassionate school policies. As someone who has been deeply engaged in period education and fostering inclusion, I have found that the AI-generated guidance includes some useful insights.

Prompt: 'How can schools support children who have started their periods, ensure inclusion, and assist with pain management?'

Supporting pupils who have started their periods is crucial to ensuring their well-being, comfort, and inclusion within the school environment. Here are some strategies that schools can adopt to provide comprehensive support to these pupils:

1   Education and awareness:

- Implement age-appropriate education about puberty, menstruation, and reproductive health for all pupils, regardless of gender.

- Foster an open and respectful environment where discussions about menstruation are normalised and free from stigma.

2   Access to menstrual supplies:

- Ensure that menstrual products (pads, tampons, etc.) are readily available in washrooms and other discreet locations throughout the school.

- Consider providing a variety of product options to accommodate individual preferences.

3 Privacy and discretion:

- Design washrooms and changing areas to provide privacy and discretion for pupils who may need to change or manage their menstrual products.
- Create a system for discreetly requesting menstrual supplies from teachers or the school nurse, if needed.

4 Pain management:

- Establish a protocol for pupils to access pain relief medication (with parental permission) if they experience menstrual pain.
- Designate a quiet and comfortable space where pupils can rest if they are experiencing discomfort.

5 Nurse's office:

- Ensure that the school nurse is knowledgeable about menstrual health and can provide guidance, information, and support to pupils.
- Create a comfortable space within the nurse's office for pupils to rest or manage their periods if needed.

6 Communication and support:

- Encourage open communication between pupils, parents, and teachers regarding menstrual health.
- Work with parents to understand any specific needs or accommodations their child may require.

7 Inclusive language and policies:

- Use inclusive language that acknowledges the diversity of gender identities and biological experiences related to menstruation.
- Develop policies that accommodate all pupils, regardless of gender identity, and ensure that these policies are communicated clearly to staff and pupils.

8 Support networks:

- Establish peer support groups or clubs where pupils can discuss and share experiences related to puberty and menstruation.
- Provide opportunities for pupils to learn from older peers who have already navigated these experiences.

9 Curriculum integration:

- Integrate discussions about menstrual health and reproductive education into the curriculum, including subjects such as science, health, and personal development.

10 Staff training:

- Provide training to teachers and staff members about supporting pupils with menstruation, including how to respond sensitively to pupils' needs.

11 Flexibility and accommodations:

- Be flexible with pupils who may need additional breaks or accommodations due to discomfort or other menstrual-related issues.
- Offer alternative options for physical education activities if needed.

12 Feedback and continuous improvement:

- Seek feedback from pupils, parents, and staff about the effectiveness of the school's support systems and make adjustments as necessary.

By implementing these strategies, schools can create a supportive and inclusive environment for pupils who have started their periods. This approach not only addresses their physical needs but also contributes to their overall well-being, comfort, and confidence within the school community.

84. Restorative Practices

During my time as a student teacher, I had a placement in a school where the policy was to handle behaviour incidents through restorative conversations. However, I hadn't covered this approach during my university studies and numerous colleagues were uncertain about it too. While it is not reasonable to assume that teachers can manage behaviour systems without adequate training, I can also envision how AI might have assisted me in navigating this situation.

Prompt: 'What is a restorative conversation and how can a teacher facilitate this with pupils?'

A restorative conversation is a structured dialogue aimed at addressing conflicts, repairing harm, and fostering understanding among individuals involved in a situation. It focuses on open communication, empathy, accountability, and collaboration to resolve issues and rebuild relationships. In an educational context, restorative conversations are a powerful tool for resolving conflicts between pupils, addressing disruptive behaviour, and promoting a positive and supportive classroom environment.

To facilitate a restorative conversation with pupils, a teacher can follow these steps:

1   Choose a suitable setting: Select a private and quiet space where everyone involved feels comfortable and safe. This environment encourages open and honest communication.

2   Prepare and plan: As the teacher, familiarise yourself with the principles of restorative conversations. Determine the main issue to be discussed and identify the individuals involved.

3   Set the tone: Create a non-judgemental atmosphere by welcoming everyone and explaining the purpose of the conversation – to listen, understand, and work together towards a resolution.

4   Share perspectives: Give each participant a chance to express their feelings, thoughts, and experiences related to the situation. Encourage active listening and empathy from all involved.

5   Use open-ended questions: Pose open-ended questions to encourage participants to reflect on their actions, motivations, and the impact of

their behaviour on others. This helps to foster self-awareness and understanding.

6 Reflective statements: Summarise what you have heard from each participant to ensure accurate understanding. This also shows that their perspectives are valued.

7 Identify harm and needs: Discuss the harm caused by the situation and explore the needs and expectations of those affected. This step encourages empathy and highlights the human impact of the conflict.

8 Problem-solving: Encourage participants to collaboratively brainstorm solutions that address the harm caused and meet the needs of everyone involved. The focus is on finding solutions rather than assigning blame.

9 Agreement and commitment: Once a solution is agreed upon, ask participants if they are comfortable with it and if they commit to following through. This step encourages accountability and ownership of the resolution.

10 Follow-up: Schedule a follow-up meeting to check on the progress and effectiveness of the agreed-upon solution. This demonstrates ongoing support and helps to maintain a positive atmosphere.

11 Closure: Conclude the conversation by expressing appreciation for participants' willingness to engage in the conversation and work towards a resolution. Reiterate the importance of maintaining respectful relationships.

Remember that restorative conversations require patience, active listening, and a non-judgemental attitude. By facilitating these conversations, teachers can create a safe and supportive learning environment where conflicts are addressed constructively, and pupils learn valuable skills for communication and conflict resolution.

AI can also help by providing further information on any points you are unclear about – for example, there were times when I felt this approach would be unsuitable.

Prompt: 'Are there examples of school incidents where a restorative conversation would not be appropriate?'

While restorative conversations are valuable tools for addressing a wide range of conflicts and incidents in a school setting, there are certain situations where they may not be the most appropriate approach. Here are a few examples:

1   Serious safety threats: In cases involving threats of violence, severe bullying, or other situations that pose an immediate danger to pupils or staff, the primary concern should be ensuring safety. Law enforcement and school authorities may need to take immediate action to address the threat before any restorative processes can be considered.

2   Repeat offences: If a pupil has repeatedly engaged in harmful behaviour, especially if it is intentional and calculated, a more comprehensive intervention may be necessary to address underlying issues. Restorative conversations might not be effective if there is a pattern of behaviour that hasn't responded to previous attempts at intervention.

3   Power imbalance: In situations where there is a significant power imbalance, such as teacher–pupil conflicts or incidents involving authority figures, the affected parties may not feel comfortable speaking openly in a restorative conversation. This could hinder the effectiveness of the process and potentially lead to further harm.

4   Serious criminal activity: Crimes of a serious nature that warrant legal action, such as theft, assault, or drug-related offences, typically fall under the jurisdiction of law enforcement and the legal system. Restorative approaches might not be appropriate until legal matters have been resolved.

5   Emotional trauma: If an incident has caused significant emotional trauma to the victim, they may not be ready or willing to participate in a restorative conversation. In such cases, individual counselling and support may be more appropriate before considering any restorative processes.

6   Ongoing systemic issues: In cases where the conflict or harm is a symptom of broader systemic issues within the school or community, addressing those underlying issues should be a priority. Restorative conversations might not adequately address deep-rooted problems that require systemic change.

It is important to note that the appropriateness of using restorative conversations depends on the specific circumstances of each incident. School administrators, counsellors, and teachers should carefully consider the nature of the incident, the needs and comfort levels of those involved, and any potential legal or safety implications before deciding whether to proceed with a restorative approach.

85. Supporting Neurodiverse Learners

AI has the potential to revolutionise education for all pupils, but neurodivergent children stand to benefit the most. By adapting to individual learning styles and strengths, AI-powered tools enable pupils to work at their own pace, which will hopefully result in more inclusive classrooms. As a dyslexic person myself, I am impressed with the following advice generated by an AI app.

Prompt: 'Can you tell me how I can support a child in my class with dyslexia?'

Certainly! Supporting a child with dyslexia in your class involves understanding their needs and implementing strategies that can help them succeed. Here are some general tips to support a child with dyslexia:

1 Educate yourself: Learn about dyslexia, its characteristics, and how it affects reading and writing skills. This will help you better understand the challenges the child may face and the strategies that can be effective.

2 Create a supportive environment: Foster a positive and inclusive classroom environment where the child feels safe and supported. Encourage empathy and understanding among classmates.

3 Provide accommodations: Offer accommodations that can help the child with dyslexia access the curriculum. This may include providing extra time for assignments and tests, allowing the use of assistive technology, or providing audio versions of texts.

4 Multisensory instruction: Use teaching methods that engage multiple senses, such as incorporating visual aids, hands-on activities, and auditory cues. This can help to reinforce learning and make it more accessible for pupils with dyslexia.

5 Differentiate instruction: Tailor your teaching to meet the individual needs of the child. Provide additional support, repetition, and reinforcement as needed. Break down complex tasks into smaller, more manageable steps.

6 Provide structured and explicit instruction: Use explicit teaching techniques that provide clear explanations, modelling, and guided practice. Break down reading and writing skills into smaller components and provide explicit instruction for each step.

7 Use assistive technology: Explore the use of assistive technology tools that can support reading and writing for pupils with dyslexia. This may

include text-to-speech software, speech recognition tools, or dyslexia-friendly fonts.

8 Collaborate with specialists: Work closely with special education teachers, reading specialists, and other professionals who can provide additional support and guidance. Collaborate on strategies and interventions to best meet the child's needs.

Remember, every child with dyslexia is unique, so it is important to regularly communicate with the child, their parents, and any specialists involved to ensure you are providing the most effective support.

Of course, you can ask AI for advice in supporting pupils with a range of learning difficulties, such as dyscalculia or dysgraphia (and, remember, we don't need a diagnosis to support a child who is struggling).

Prompt: 'Can you tell me how to support a pupil in my class with dyscalculia?'

Supporting a pupil with dyscalculia, a specific learning disability related to maths, requires a combination of understanding, patience, and targeted interventions. Here are some strategies to support a pupil with dyscalculia in your class:

1 Early identification and assessment: Collaborate with the school's special education team or a learning specialist to ensure the pupil is properly assessed for dyscalculia. Early identification is crucial for effective support.

2 Individualised education plan (IEP): Work with the pupil's IEP team to develop a personalised plan that outlines their specific needs, goals, and accommodations.

3 Use multisensory approaches: Incorporate multisensory teaching methods whenever possible. This can include using manipulatives (like counting blocks), visual aids, and tactile materials to help the pupil understand mathematical concepts.

4 Break down concepts: Break down complex maths concepts into smaller, more manageable steps. Provide step-by-step instructions and opportunities for the pupil to practise each step before moving on.

5   Repetition and consistency: Provide ample opportunities for practice and review of previously learned concepts. Consistency in teaching methods and routines can be reassuring for the pupil.

6   Visual aids and diagrams: Use visual aids such as charts, diagrams, and colour-coding to help illustrate mathematical concepts. Visual representations can make abstract ideas more concrete.

7   Real-life applications: Relate maths concepts to real-life situations whenever possible. This helps the pupil to see the practical relevance of what they are learning.

8   Alternative assessments: Be open to alternative methods of assessment. Consider allowing the pupil to demonstrate their understanding through oral presentations, projects, or other non-written methods.

9   Extra time and support: Provide extra time for completing maths assignments and tests. Offer one-on-one support or small group sessions if necessary.

10 Positive reinforcement and encouragement: Recognise and praise the pupil's efforts and progress, no matter how small. Encouragement can boost their confidence and motivation.

11 Peer support and group work: Encourage peer support and group work, where the pupil can learn from their classmates. Assigning a maths buddy can be beneficial.

12 Regular communication: Maintain open communication with the pupil's parents or caregivers to update them on progress and discuss strategies for support at home.

13 Professional development: Stay informed about dyscalculia and best practices in teaching maths to pupils with learning disabilities through professional development opportunities.

14 Flexibility and patience: Be patient and flexible with the pupil. Recognise that progress may be slow, and different strategies may need to be tried before finding what works best.

15 Advocate for the pupil: Advocate for the pupil's needs within the school system, ensuring that they receive the appropriate accommodations and support outlined in their IEP.

Remember that every pupil with dyscalculia is unique, and what works for one may not work for another. It is essential to continuously assess the pupil's progress and adjust your support strategies accordingly. Additionally, involving parents and collaborating with special education professionals can greatly benefit the pupil's overall development.

86. Creating Staff Well-Being Policies

I believe that teachers are inherently creative individuals with a strong vision. Often, we come up with fantastic ideas that could enrich the overall school experience. Yet, all too frequently, time constraints, resource limitations, bureaucratic obstacles, and sheer exhaustion hinder our progress. AI offers an opportunity to streamline the process of devising policies with the potential to improve the well-being of school staff.

One common observation, particularly in the primary sector where women dominate the profession, is that numerous schools and employers lack policies that are relevant to our specific needs. This is an area where advocating for inclusive policies can make a substantial difference in addressing these disparities. To pick just one example, does your school have a menopause policy? If not, you can use AI to help you create one.

Prompt: 'Create a policy to support school staff with menopause.'

School Staff Menopause Support Policy

Policy Statement:

Our school recognises the importance of creating a supportive and inclusive environment for all staff members, including those who may be experiencing the challenges of menopause. This policy aims to provide guidance, resources, and accommodations to ensure that staff going through menopause can continue to thrive in their roles.

Objectives:

1   Awareness and education: Raise awareness about menopause among staff and promote a better understanding of its physical and emotional impact.

2   Open communication: Encourage open conversations and destigmatise discussions related to menopause to create an environment where staff feel comfortable seeking support.

3   Flexible working arrangements: Offer flexible working arrangements to accommodate the varying needs of staff experiencing menopause-related symptoms.

4   Physical comfort: Provide access to temperature control, proper ventilation, and comfortable seating arrangements to help manage common symptoms such as hot flashes.

5   Access to information: Ensure staff have access to reliable information about menopause and its impact, as well as resources for managing symptoms.

6   Health and well-being: Promote well-being by offering opportunities for stress management, exercise, and healthy lifestyle choices.

7   Supportive leave: Provide paid or unpaid leave options for staff who require time off due to severe menopause symptoms or medical appointments.

8   Confidentiality and dignity: Ensure that discussions about menopause-related issues are handled confidentially and with respect for individual dignity.

Implementation:

1   Awareness campaigns: Conduct workshops, seminars, or informational sessions about menopause to educate staff and dispel misconceptions.

2   Designated support person: Appoint a designated staff member or team to be a point of contact for staff seeking information, advice, or support related to menopause.

3   Flexible work arrangements: Work with individual staff members to establish flexible schedules, reduced workload, or remote work options, if feasible.

4   Physical comfort: Maintain a comfortable and adjustable environment, including temperature control and suitable seating, in common workspaces.

5   Resource centre: Establish a resource centre or online portal with reliable information, self-care tips, and links to external support networks.

6   Well-being initiatives: Introduce well-being programmes, such as yoga, mindfulness sessions, and fitness classes, which can help to alleviate menopause symptoms.

7   Leave policy: Develop a specific leave policy that addresses the unique needs of staff experiencing menopause, including paid and unpaid leave options.

8   Confidentiality guidelines: Establish guidelines for staff and supervisors on how to handle conversations and requests related to menopause, emphasising confidentiality.

Review and evaluation:

The effectiveness of this policy will be periodically reviewed through staff feedback, surveys, and ongoing monitoring of its implementation. Adjustments will be made based on the evolving needs and requirements of staff experiencing menopause.

This policy aims to create a workplace culture that supports staff members during the menopausal transition, ensuring their well-being, comfort, and continued professional growth.

There might be similar policies absent from your workplace, perhaps relating to menstruation, adoption leave, support for staff undergoing fertility treatment, miscarriage, and abortion leave. You can utilise AI to assist in creating them too. This technology has the capacity to make improvements in staff and pupil well-being by taking on burdensome tasks that we might not get round to due to time constraints.

If you hold a leadership position, you might have the opportunity to implement policies that bring about positive change. However, if you aren't in a leadership role, there is nothing stopping you from suggesting policies and advocating for them within your school or trade union. You can work to put these ideas into practice at a school, local, or even national level.

87. Staff Well-Being Initiatives

While AI can reduce your workload and improve efficiency in schools, there is always the potential for further improvement. According to Education Support's Teacher Wellbeing Index, 78% of staff report experiencing mental health symptoms due to their work.[8] If you hold a leadership position, you can employ an AI-generated checklist to evaluate how well your school is supporting staff well-being. For those not in leadership roles, proposing proactive ideas to the management team is a viable approach.

Prompt: 'Suggest ways that schools can improve teacher well-being.'

1   Workload management: Ensure that teachers have reasonable workloads by setting realistic expectations and providing sufficient planning time. Encourage collaboration to share best practices and resources.

2   Professional development: Offer ongoing professional development opportunities that align with teachers' interests and career goals. This can boost their sense of growth and accomplishment.

3   Mentorship and support: Establish mentorship programmes where experienced teachers provide guidance and support to newer colleagues. This helps to create a sense of community and reduces feelings of isolation.

4   Autonomy and decision-making: Allow teachers to have a say in curriculum development, teaching methods, and classroom management. Empowering them with autonomy fosters a sense of ownership and satisfaction.

5   Positive school culture: Cultivate a positive and inclusive school culture that promotes teamwork, open communication, and mutual respect. Celebrate teachers' successes and contributions.

6   Wellness programmes: Offer wellness programmes such as yoga classes, mindfulness sessions, or access to mental health resources. Encourage healthy habits and stress management techniques.

7   Flexible work arrangements: Provide flexible work arrangements when possible, such as opportunities for remote work or adjusted schedules. This can help to accommodate teachers' personal needs.

8   See https://www.educationsupport.org.uk/resources/for-organisations/research/teacher-wellbeing-index.

8   Recognition and appreciation: Regularly acknowledge and appreciate teachers' efforts and achievements. Celebrate milestones, birthdays, and accomplishments to foster a sense of value.

9   Clear communication: Keep teachers informed about school policies, changes, and decisions. Transparent communication helps to reduce uncertainty and stress.

10 Collaborative planning: Encourage collaborative lesson planning, sharing of resources, and co-teaching opportunities. This promotes a sense of unity and shared responsibility.

11 Reduced administrative tasks: Minimise administrative tasks that do not directly contribute to teaching and learning. Streamline processes to free up teachers' time for instructional activities.

12 Access to resources: Ensure that teachers have access to necessary teaching materials, technology, and resources. This reduces frustration and helps them to focus on teaching.

13 Regular feedback: Provide constructive feedback on teaching performance and classroom management. This helps teachers to improve and grow in their roles.

14 Healthy work–life balance: Encourage a healthy work–life balance by discouraging excessive overtime and promoting the importance of rest and personal time.

15 Conflict resolution: Establish effective mechanisms for conflict resolution, should any arise among staff. A supportive environment helps to maintain positive relationships.

By prioritising teacher well-being, schools can create a nurturing and productive environment that not only benefits teachers but also positively impacts pupils' learning experiences.

AI can give suggestions at a staffroom level too to lift spirits and foster camaraderie: 'Suggest ideas that teachers can do for each other to boost morale – for example, staffroom break ideas.'

1   Gratitude notes: Leave anonymous or personalised gratitude notes for colleagues, expressing appreciation for their hard work and contributions.

2   Morning boost: Organise a rotating schedule for teachers to bring in breakfast treats, such as bagels, pastries, or fruit, to share with the staff.

3   Inspiring quotes: Create a 'Quote of the Day' board in the staffroom with uplifting and motivational quotes that teachers can read and reflect on.

4   Tea and coffee station: Set up a self-serve tea and coffee station with a variety of options and cosy additions like flavoured syrups, whipped cream, and marshmallows.

5   Themed dress-up days: Coordinate fun dress-up themes for certain days of the week, like 'Favourite Colour Day' or 'Mismatched Sock Day', to add a touch of whimsy.

6   Book exchange: Create a mini-library of books that teachers can borrow and enjoy during their breaks, fostering a love for reading.

7   Joke or riddle board: Create a bulletin board with a collection of jokes, riddles, and puns to bring smiles and laughter to the staffroom.

8   Celebration corner: Dedicate a corner for celebrating colleagues' birthdays, work anniversaries, and personal accomplishments with small decorations and treats.

9   Wellness breaks: Organise brief mindfulness or relaxation sessions during breaks, where teachers can practise deep breathing or stretching exercises.

10 Recipe swap: Share and exchange simple, healthy snack recipes that teachers can prepare and enjoy during their breaks.

11 Lunch potluck: Plan a monthly potluck where teachers can bring homemade dishes to share during lunch, promoting culinary diversity and bonding.

12 Plant exchange: Arrange a plant exchange where teachers can bring in potted plants or succulents to swap, adding a touch of greenery to the staffroom.

13 Themed trivia: Host a trivia game during breaks with themes related to pop culture, history, or general knowledge to engage and entertain.

14 Mindfulness colouring: Provide colouring pages and coloured pencils for teachers to engage in relaxing colouring activities during breaks.

15 Compliment box: Set up a box for teachers to leave anonymous compliments for their colleagues, fostering positivity and boosting self-esteem.

16 Photo collage: Create a photo collage showcasing memorable moments from school events, field trips, and other enjoyable activities.

17 Supportive affirmations: Craft positive affirmations on sticky notes and place them on colleagues' desks to provide encouragement and motivation.

Remember, even small acts of kindness and positivity can have a significant impact on morale. Encourage a culture of appreciation and support among staff members, enhancing the overall well-being of the school community.

88. Awareness Days

Although we should aim to embed inclusion into every aspect of school life, awareness days (or weeks or months) offer a great opportunity to raise the profile of important issues or topics.

Prompt: 'Can you give me a list of awareness days from January to July?'

Here is a list of awareness days and observances from January to July. Please note that this list includes a wide range of topics and may not be exhaustive. Additionally, awareness days can vary by country, so this list may not cover all observances in your specific region:

January:

1 New Year's Day (1 January)

2 World Braille Day (4 January)

3 International Day of Education (24 January)

4 Data Privacy Day (28 January)

February:

5 World Wetlands Day (2 February)

6 World Cancer Day (4 February)

7 Safer Internet Day (8 February)

8 International Day of Women and Girls in Science (11 February)

9 Valentine's Day (14 February)

10 World Day of Social Justice (20 February)

March:

11 World Wildlife Day (3 March)

12 International Women's Day (8 March)

13 International Day of Happiness (20 March)

14 World Water Day (22 March)

15 Earth Hour (last Saturday of March)

April:

16 World Autism Awareness Day (2 April)

17 World Health Day (7 April)

18 Earth Day (22 April)

19 World Malaria Day (25 April)

20 International Dance Day (29 April)

May:

21 International Labour Day (1 May)

22 World Press Freedom Day (3 May)

23 Global Accessibility Awareness Day (20 May)

24 World No Tobacco Day (31 May)

June:

25 World Environment Day (5 June)

26 World Oceans Day (8 June)

27 World Blood Donor Day (14 June)

28 World Refugee Day (20 June)

29 International Day of Yoga (21 June)

30 International Day Against Drug Abuse and Illicit Trafficking (26 June)

July:

31 World Population Day (11 July)

32 Nelson Mandela International Day (18 July)

33 World Hepatitis Day (28 July)

34 International Tiger Day (29 July)

35 International Day of Friendship (30 July)

This list provides a glimpse of some of the many awareness days and observances that occur throughout the year. You can find more specific and region-specific awareness days by searching online or referring to official websites related to specific causes or issues.

If you decide to do some learning on International Women's Day, for example, you can use AI to help you with planning a lesson or whole-school assembly.

Prompt: 'Plan a lesson for Key Stage 2 on International Women's Day.'

Celebrating International Women's Day

Objective: To introduce children to the concept of International Women's Day, explore the importance of gender equality, and celebrate the achievements of women throughout history.

Materials:

- Whiteboard and markers
- Visual aids (images of notable women from different fields)
- Stories or biographies about influential women
- Arts and craft supplies (optional)
- Internet access for research (optional)

Duration: approximately 45–60 minutes

1   Introduction (15 minutes):

- Begin by asking the pupils if they have ever heard of International Women's Day and what they think it might be about. Discuss their thoughts briefly.

- Explain that International Women's Day is a global celebration of the social, economic, cultural, and political achievements of women. It also serves as a reminder of the ongoing work needed to achieve gender equality.

- Share some historical background, such as the origins of International Women's Day on 8 March and its significance. Discuss the theme for the current year, if available.

2   Activities (20 minutes):

- Show images of notable women from various fields, including science, literature, sports, and politics. Discuss their achievements and the impact they have had on the world.

- Read or share short stories or biographies about some of these women. Encourage pupils to ask questions and express their thoughts.

- Discuss the importance of gender equality and why it is important to recognise the accomplishments of women. Highlight that International Women's Day is not just for celebrating women but also for promoting equality.

3 Presentations (10 minutes):

- Have pupils choose a woman they find inspiring or research one on their own. They can create a poster or a brief presentation to share with the class on why they admire this woman and what they have learned about her.

4 Conclusion (10 minutes):

- Allow pupils to present their posters or presentations if time permits.
- Conclude by summarising the key points:
  - International Women's Day celebrates women's achievements.
  - Gender equality is important, and everyone should have equal opportunities.
  - We can all learn from the accomplishments of remarkable women.
- Encourage pupils to think about ways they can promote gender equality in their own lives.

Homework (optional):

- For homework, ask pupils to interview a woman in their life (e.g. a family member, friend, or teacher) about her achievements and any challenges she has faced. They can share what they learn in the next class.

Extension activity (optional):

- For a longer project, pupils can research and create a presentation on a specific issue related to gender equality and present it to the class on a future date.

Assessment:

- Assess pupils based on their participation in class discussions, the quality of their poster or presentation, and their understanding of the importance of International Women's Day and gender equality.

As we have seen, AI can default to white, heteronormative, and ableist narratives; however, it can be a useful tool for promoting inclusion, if we give it precise requests. With that in mind, AI can be further prompted: 'Provide a biography for a disabled woman for the above lesson.' In this instance, AI provided a biography of Mexican artist Frida Kahlo.

89. Supporting Neurodiverse Teachers

As a dyslexic teacher, I am aware that I have the option to request 'reasonable adjustments' in the workplace. However, it can be difficult to determine where to begin, what to request, and what is considered 'reasonable', especially when every aspect of work feels crucial. Individuals in leadership positions are faced with a similar dilemma.

Most schools work hard to develop policies and structures that support children with additional needs, but less attention is paid to neurodiverse members of staff. AI can play a role in providing recommendations to school leaders. Naturally, individual needs vary and the solutions that benefit one person may not necessarily be effective for another. Nevertheless, the following suggestions can serve as a helpful starting point.

Prompt: 'What reasonable adjustments could be made at work for a school teacher who is dyslexic?'

Reasonable adjustments for a school teacher with dyslexia can greatly enhance their ability to perform their job effectively. Dyslexia can affect reading, writing, spelling, and sometimes organisational skills. Here are some reasonable adjustments that can be made to support a dyslexic teacher:

1   Flexible reading and writing expectations: Modify the amount of written work required from the teacher. Allow for alternatives to written reports or assignments, such as verbal presentations or recorded videos.

2   Assistive technology: Provide access to assistive technology like speech-to-text software (e.g. Dragon NaturallySpeaking) and text-to-speech software (e.g. Read&Write). These tools can help with writing and reading tasks.

3   Extended time for tasks: Allow extra time for lesson planning, grading, and administrative tasks that involve reading and writing. This extra time can help to reduce stress and improve the quality of work.

4   Prepared materials: Provide lesson plans, worksheets, and other instructional materials in advance to give the teacher more time to review and prepare. This can help them to familiarise themselves with the content and make any necessary adjustments.

5   Proofreading support: Offer access to a proofreading assistant who can help review written materials, including emails, announcements, and

lesson plans, to catch any errors before they are shared with pupils, parents, or colleagues.

6   Colour-coded organisational systems: Use colour-coding for materials, folders, and schedules to help the teacher better organise and locate resources.

7   Visual aids: Utilise visual aids, diagrams, and charts in teaching materials to help convey information in different formats.

8   Simplified instructions: Present instructions and information in clear, concise language, avoiding jargon or complex sentence structures.

9   Flexible assessment methods: Allow the teacher to use alternative methods for assessing pupils, such as oral presentations, project-based assessments, or video assignments.

10 Quiet workspace: Provide a quiet and well-organised workspace for lesson planning and grading to minimise distractions.

11 Professional development: Offer workshops and training on dyslexia awareness, teaching strategies, and assistive technologies to help the teacher continuously improve their skills.

12 Collaborative planning: Encourage collaborative planning with colleagues, where ideas and materials can be shared, reducing the individual workload.

13 Positive feedback and encouragement: Recognise the teacher's strengths and efforts, providing regular feedback and encouragement.

14 Flexible scheduling: If possible, adjust the teacher's schedule to accommodate their peak cognitive hours, when they may find tasks like reading and writing easier.

15 Open communication: Maintain an open line of communication with the teacher to understand their needs and preferences. Regular check-ins can help to ensure that adjustments are effective and relevant.

Remember that the specific adjustments needed may vary based on the individual's preferences and strengths. It is essential to engage in an interactive dialogue with the teacher to determine the most suitable accommodations that will enable them to perform their role effectively.

As with pupils, we can use information and suggestions from AI to support teachers who have a range of disabilities in the workplace.

90. CV Building and Applications

While I am not suggesting using AI to write job applications for you, applying for jobs is a time-consuming process and AI can be used for inspiration (and to proofread your answers). Here are some questions from a current teaching vacancy and what AI produces in response.

Please add a brief description of responsibilities, experience and knowledge gained.

In my role as a primary teacher, I have taken on a diverse range of responsibilities aimed at nurturing young minds and creating a positive learning environment. With [X] years of experience, I have gained valuable insights and knowledge that have further enriched my teaching practices.

Responsibilities:

- Planning and delivering engaging lessons that cater to various learning styles and abilities.

- Creating a supportive and inclusive classroom atmosphere that encourages active participation and cooperation.

- Assessing pupils' progress through continuous observation, formal assessments, and interactive activities.

- Collaborating with fellow teachers, parents, and school staff to enhance the overall learning experience.

- Designing and implementing creative teaching aids and resources to enhance pupil understanding.

- Addressing individual learning needs by tailoring instruction and providing additional support where required.

- Fostering pupils' personal and social development through structured activities and open discussions.

- Organising and supervising extracurricular activities, field trips, and events to enrich pupils' educational experience.

Experience:

Throughout my tenure as a primary teacher, I have had the privilege of working with pupils aged [X to Y], enabling me to adapt my teaching methods effectively to each developmental stage. I have cultivated a classroom environment that promotes curiosity, critical thinking, and a love for learning. Through hands-on projects, interactive learning, and group activities, I have witnessed pupils grow not only academically but also as confident and socially aware individuals.

Knowledge gained:

My experience as a primary teacher has deepened my understanding of child psychology, pedagogical strategies, and classroom management techniques. I have honed my ability to differentiate instruction, tailoring lessons to accommodate diverse learning needs. I have gained insights into fostering a culture of respect, empathy, and teamwork among pupils. Additionally, I have acquired a strong grasp of curriculum design, assessment methods, and the importance of adapting teaching techniques to the digital age.

Overall, my journey as a primary teacher has equipped me with a well-rounded skill set, a passion for fostering young minds, and a commitment to creating a positive and nurturing educational environment.

Professional knowledge and understanding – curriculum and pedagogy. Outline your professional knowledge and understanding of curriculum delivery taking into account the responsibility of all elements: literacy, numeracy, health and well-being.

My professional knowledge and understanding of curriculum delivery reflect a comprehensive approach that prioritises the holistic development of pupils. As a primary teacher, I recognise the significance of catering to the diverse needs of learners across different subjects, including literacy, numeracy, health, and well-being.

Literacy:

I possess a deep understanding of literacy development, encompassing reading, writing, listening, and speaking skills. I am well-versed in employing a variety of teaching methodologies, such as phonics instruction, guided reading, and interactive writing, to ensure that pupils become confident communicators. By fostering a literature-rich classroom environment and incorporating both classic and contemporary texts, I encourage pupils to explore their imagination and critical thinking skills while strengthening their language proficiency.

Numeracy:

My approach to numeracy emphasises the importance of conceptual understanding alongside procedural fluency. I employ hands-on activities, problem-solving tasks, and real-life scenarios to make mathematical concepts tangible and relatable. My experience in differentiating instruction allows me to address varying levels of mathematical readiness, ensuring that all pupils can progress at their own pace. I believe in building a strong foundation in numeracy skills, enabling pupils to think critically and apply mathematical principles in practical situations.

Health and well-being:

Recognising the integral role of health and well-being in a pupil's overall development, I have a comprehensive grasp of promoting physical, emotional, and social wellness in the classroom. I integrate activities that cultivate emotional intelligence, empathy, and resilience. Through collaborative projects, discussions, and mindfulness practices, I create a safe and supportive environment where pupils can express themselves, develop healthy relationships, and navigate challenges with confidence.

In summary, my professional knowledge and understanding of curriculum delivery align with a pupil-centred approach that encompasses literacy, numeracy, health, and well-being. I believe in nurturing not only academic excellence but also the holistic growth of each pupil, equipping them with the skills and attitudes they need to succeed both inside and outside the classroom.

91. Continuing Professional Development

As teachers, it is an integral part of our job to keep our CPD current and well-documented. AI can serve as a helpful tool in this endeavour, whether that is sourcing information, suggesting pertinent research, or summarising relevant documents.

For example, I queried AI to discover 'New research areas in primary education' to find out how AI can contribute to professional growth.

Some potential new research areas in primary education include:

1   Technology integration and digital literacy: Exploring how to effectively integrate technology into primary classrooms and how to develop digital literacy skills among young learners. This includes understanding the impact of educational apps, online resources, and remote learning environments on primary education.

2   Socio-emotional learning: Investigating how to integrate social and emotional learning into primary education to enhance pupils' well-being, resilience, and interpersonal skills. This includes strategies for teaching empathy, self-awareness, and emotional regulation.

3   Inclusive education: Focusing on strategies to create more inclusive classrooms that accommodate diverse learning needs and backgrounds. This could involve researching the effectiveness of different instructional methods and classroom arrangements to ensure all pupils thrive.

4   Multilingualism and language acquisition: Examining how primary pupils acquire and develop language skills, especially in multilingual or multicultural contexts. Research in this area might explore the benefits of bilingual education, strategies for supporting English language learners, and the role of culture in language acquisition.

5   Project-based and enquiry-based learning: Studying the effectiveness of project-based learning and enquiry-based learning approaches in primary classrooms. This includes understanding how these approaches foster critical thinking, problem-solving skills, and a deeper understanding of content.

6   Environmental and sustainability education: Investigating how to incorporate environmental and sustainability education into primary curricula. Research might focus on designing age-appropriate activities,

measuring the impact of such education on pupils' attitudes and behaviours, and assessing the role of schools in promoting sustainability.

7 Assessment for learning: Exploring innovative assessment methods that focus on formative assessment and feedback to guide pupil learning. Research might involve evaluating the effectiveness of alternative assessment techniques that go beyond traditional testing.

8 Neuroeducation and cognitive development: Studying how insights from neuroscience can inform primary education practices. This could involve understanding the cognitive development of young learners and adapting teaching methods accordingly.

9 Parent and community involvement: Researching effective strategies for involving parents and the community in primary education. This includes investigating how partnerships between schools, families, and local organisations can enhance pupil achievement and well-being.

Remember that the field of education is dynamic and always evolving. New research areas might emerge as educational practices, technology, and societal needs change. To get the most up-to-date information on new research trends in primary education, I recommend checking recent academic journals, educational conferences, and publications from reputable educational research organisations.

You might want to drill down into a research area that interests you. Prompt: 'Can you tell me more about social and emotional learning?'

Social and emotional learning (SEL) refers to the process of acquiring and applying the skills, attitudes, and knowledge necessary for understanding and managing emotions, developing positive relationships, making responsible decisions, and effectively navigating various social contexts. SEL is an essential aspect of education that goes beyond academic content and focuses on the holistic development of pupils' emotional well-being and social competence.

Key components of SEL:

1 Self-awareness: This involves recognising and understanding one's own emotions, strengths, and limitations. Pupils learn to accurately identify their feelings, emotions, and reactions in different situations.

2 Self-management: Self-management entails regulating one's emotions, impulses, and behaviours. Pupils learn strategies to handle stress, control

impulses, and set goals. This component helps pupils to develop self-discipline and effective strategies for managing their emotions.

3 Social awareness: Social awareness involves understanding and empathising with the emotions and perspectives of others. Pupils develop the ability to appreciate diversity, demonstrate empathy, and navigate various social situations with respect and understanding.

4 Relationship skills: This component focuses on building and maintaining healthy relationships with peers, teachers, family members, and the community. Pupils learn effective communication, active listening, conflict resolution, and cooperation skills.

5 Responsible decision-making: Pupils learn to make thoughtful and ethical decisions by considering the potential consequences of their actions. They develop critical thinking skills and learn to evaluate choices based on personal values and the well-being of themselves and others.

And then follow this up with additional research: 'Can you recommend further (UK) reading on social and emotional learning?'

Books:

- *Social and Emotional Learning: A Critical Appraisal* by Dennis M. McInerney and David Grossman: This book provides a critical analysis of SEL programmes and their effectiveness in the UK and other contexts.

- *A Little Guide to Children's Well-Being* by Roise O'Sullivan: Focused on well-being, this book provides practical guidance for teachers and parents on promoting emotional and social development in children.

- *Emotional Health and Well-Being: A Practical Guide for Schools* by Tina Rae: This book is a practical guide for educators in the UK on promoting emotional health and well-being in schools.

- *Social and Emotional Education: An International Analysis* edited by Simon C. Hunter, Sue Abbott, and Debi Roker: While it includes international perspectives, this book explores the development and implementation of SEL programmes in the UK.

- *Promoting Emotional Education: Engaging Children and Young People with Social, Emotional and Behavioral Difficulties* by Carmel Cefai and

Paul Cooper: This book offers strategies for educators dealing with pupils facing social, emotional, and behavioural difficulties in the UK.

- *The Teacher's Introduction to Attachment: Practical Essentials for Teachers, Carers, and School Support Staff* by Nicola Marshall: Attachment theory is crucial to SEL, and this book provides guidance on understanding and working with attachment in a UK educational context.

Websites and organisations:

- PSHE Association – https://pshe-association.org.uk: The PSHE Association (personal, social, health, and economic education) in the UK offers a wide range of resources, publications, and research on SEL. Their website is a valuable source for staying updated on SEL in the UK.

- British Educational Research Association – https://www.bera.ac.uk: BERA often publishes research papers and articles related to education, including SEL. Keep an eye on their publications for the latest research in the UK.

- Edutopia: Social and Emotional Learning – www.edutopia.org/topic/social-emotional-learning: A website founded by the filmmaker George Lucas to improve full-time education.

- Yale Center for Emotional Intelligence – https://medicine.yale.edu/childstudy/services/community-and-schools-programs/center-for-emotional-intelligence: The YCEI designs and researches evidence-based approaches to support school communities in developing children's emotional intelligence.

These resources can provide you with a solid foundation in understanding SEL and offer practical strategies for integrating SEL principles into your educational practice. Additionally, many academic databases and educational websites offer articles and research related to SEL that can further deepen your understanding of this important topic.

AI can produce recommended book lists across a wide range of pedagogical areas as well as summaries of each title to help you decide which ones interest you.

92. Report Comments

AI can be helpful when writing school reports. At a basic level, you can simply ask it to proofread your comments or 'check grammar and improve' (just beware of Americanised spelling; you can always ask it to use English spelling). The most time-consuming part is thinking how to word something or finding different ways to say similar things about children who are alike. AI technology can assist you to find alternative phrasings and ensure that you are wording your remarks in a respectful way.

For example, 'Give me positive report comments to write about a very quiet child' will quickly generate an extensive list:

1   The pupil is a great listener and consistently demonstrates excellent focus during class activities.

2   The pupil's quiet nature allows them to observe and absorb information effectively, leading to thoughtful contributions when they feel comfortable.

3   The pupil's calm and quiet demeanour creates a peaceful and respectful learning environment for their peers.

4   The pupil's quiet nature does not hinder their ability to actively participate in class discussions when given the opportunity.

5   The pupil's quiet demeanour allows them to work independently and complete tasks with great attention to detail.

6   The pupil's quiet nature is often accompanied by a strong sense of self-discipline, which positively influences their work ethic.

7   The pupil's quietness should not be mistaken for disengagement; they consistently demonstrate a deep understanding of the material.

8   The pupil's quiet nature allows them to be a great team player, as they actively listen to their peers and contribute meaningfully when necessary.

9   The pupil's quietness is often accompanied by a strong sense of empathy, as they are attentive to the needs and feelings of others.

10 The pupil's quiet demeanour is an asset in group work situations, as they are able to effectively collaborate and respect the ideas of their peers.

93. Easy Letters to Parents

AI can be useful with another task that can take up a lot of time – communicating with parents. For example, my school policy requires me to write to parents if I plan to show a parental guidance (PG) film in class.

For example, if I have been doing a novel study with my class on the book *Wonder* and, afterwards, I want my pupils to watch the film and compare it to the book, I will need to send a note advising parents that I plan to show a PG-rated film and to contact me if they have any concerns. AI makes this easy!

Upcoming Film Viewing: *Wonder* – Parental Notice and Open Communication

Dear Parents/Guardians,

I hope this letter finds you well. I am writing to inform you about an upcoming event related to our ongoing novel study on *Wonder*. As a part of our exploration of this meaningful story, I am planning to show the PG-rated film adaptation in class.

The film *Wonder* is a heart-warming and thought-provoking adaptation of the novel we have been studying. It beautifully captures the themes and messages we have been discussing in our class. Watching the film will provide the pupils with an opportunity to see the characters and their experiences come to life on screen.

I understand that, as parents, you might have concerns or questions about the content of the film. Your child's comfort and emotional well-being are of utmost importance to me. If you have any concerns about your child watching the film, or if you would like more information about its content, please do not hesitate to contact me. I am more than happy to address any questions or considerations you may have.

My intention is to create a positive and enriching educational experience for all pupils. If any pupil has particular sensitivities or reasons they should not view the film, please let me know confidentially so I can make appropriate arrangements.

The viewing of the film is scheduled for [Date] during our regular class hours. If you would prefer your child not to watch the film, please let me know in writing or via email before [Date].

Thank you for your continued support and cooperation. I value our partnership in providing the best learning opportunities for your child. Together, we can ensure that our pupils engage with this important story in a way that is comfortable and meaningful for them.

Looking forward to your understanding and cooperation.

Warm regards,

[Your Name]

[Your Contact Information]

94. Summarising Documents

AI offers the incredibly valuable facility of condensing lengthy documents into concise summaries. Consider the example of an exhaustive piece of government guidance; AI can swiftly transform it into a manageable précis (although I am certainly not suggesting that you should avoid reading the entire document).

Similarly, AI can be a tremendous asset when faced with the task of digesting education journal articles. It is particularly useful for individuals engaged in further studies or academic research. By harnessing AI, you can efficiently sift through a multitude of papers, identifying the ones that warrant a more thorough read and deserve referencing. This is a game-changer in the assimilation of complex information.

For example, you can copy and paste the Department for Education's document *Mathematics Guidance: Key Stages 1 and 2*[9] into an AI app and ask for a summary. (Certain applications allow you to directly upload a PDF (e.g. ChatGPT), while others simplify the process by enabling you to copy and paste a URL link.) Here is the summary:

> The document titled *Maths Guidance: Introduction* is a publication by the UK government. It provides an overview of the guidance for teaching mathematics in primary schools. The guidance aims to support teachers in delivering high-quality mathematics education to pupils. It emphasises the importance of developing a deep understanding of mathematical concepts and skills, as well as promoting problem-solving and reasoning abilities. The document highlights the key principles and approaches that should be adopted in teaching mathematics, such as using manipulatives, providing opportunities for mathematical talk, and ensuring progression in learning. It also emphasises the need for teachers to have subject knowledge and confidence in teaching mathematics effectively. The document concludes by highlighting the importance of assessment and feedback in supporting pupils' progress in mathematics.

---

9   Department for Education, *Mathematics Guidance: Key Stages 1 and 2. Non-Statutory Guidance for the National Curriculum in England: Introduction* (June 2020). Available at: https://www.gov.uk/government/publications/teaching-mathematics-in-primary-schools.

95. Risk Assessments

There is a regrettable culture of blame in many workplaces today, but AI can come to your aid even here. Teachers often need to perform risk assessments, whether for a school trip or when using classroom equipment, which can be time-consuming. However, AI can step in not only to speed up the process but also to deliver a comprehensive risk assessment that can alleviate any fear of an oversight.

Let's take the No-Bake Cookies in Activity 29 as an example. Once I have generated the recipe, I merely type in, 'Can you provide a risk assessment?'

No-Bake Chocolate Banana Oat Cookies – Risk Assessment

Hazard	Risk level	Control measures
Risk of allergies	Moderate	Ask participants if they have any allergies to ingredients like bananas, oats, cocoa, nuts, or milk. If any allergies are identified, provide alternative ingredients or choose a different recipe.
Food contamination	Low	Ensure all utensils and containers used are clean and properly washed. Participants should wash their hands before handling ingredients.
Choking hazard	Low	Advise participants to avoid putting too much mixture in their mouths at once and to take small bites. If including optional add-ins like nuts or dried fruit, ensure they are chopped finely to reduce choking risk.

Hazard	Risk level	Control measures
Burns or scalds (if using warm ingredients)	Low	If you are warming ingredients like honey or nut butter, remind participants to be cautious when handling warm substances and to avoid touching hot surfaces.
Cross-contamination (allergens)	Low	If using shared utensils and equipment, ensure they are thoroughly cleaned and sanitised to prevent cross-contamination of allergens.
Slips, trips, and falls	Low	Ensure the cooking area is well organised and free of obstacles. Keep the floor dry to prevent slips.
Cuts or injuries from utensils	Low	Provide child-safe utensils when involving children in the preparation. Ensure proper supervision.

Remember that this risk assessment is a general guideline. It is important to consider the specific circumstances of your environment, the age of participants, and any additional factors that might affect safety. Always prioritise safety and supervision when involving children in cooking activities.

AI offers a solution to the demanding task of risk assessment, giving teachers confidence in classroom safety measures and therefore allowing them to focus on providing enriching learning experiences.

96. Parent Information Leaflets

AI apps and websites can effortlessly produce information documents for you to send home to parents informing them about the measures the school is implementing to tackle pupil well-being or bullying issues. For example, in the last few years, schools have seen a rise in cyberbullying. Although most of these incidents occur outside school, nonetheless, schools can support pupils by talking to them about cyber safety and bullying and by providing information for parents.

Prompt: 'Write a parent information leaflet explaining that there have been cyberbullying incidents in class and detailing what they can do to help.'

Parent Information Leaflet: Addressing Cyberbullying in the Classroom

Dear Parents and Guardians,

We hope this message finds you well. We want to address an important issue that has come to our attention – cyberbullying within our classroom community. Our primary concern is the well-being and safety of all our pupils, and we believe that with your partnership, we can create a positive and secure online environment for every child.

What is cyberbullying?

Cyberbullying involves the use of digital communication tools such as social media, messaging apps, and online platforms to intimidate, harass, or embarrass others. This type of bullying can cause emotional distress, affect self-esteem, and impact a child's overall mental health.

Signs your child might be affected:

- Changes in behaviour, mood, or academic performance.
- Avoidance of using devices or participating in online activities.
- Unwillingness to discuss online interactions or discomfort when the topic is raised.

How you can help:

1 Open communication: Establish a safe space where your child feels comfortable discussing their online experiences. Encourage them to share both positive and negative encounters.

2   Educate: Discuss the importance of treating others with kindness and respect both online and offline. Teach your child about the impact of their words and actions on others.

3   Monitor online activities: Regularly check your child's online interactions without invading their privacy. Encourage them to share concerns if they experience or witness cyberbullying.

4   Set privacy settings: Help your child to understand the importance of privacy settings on their devices and social media accounts. Explain how to block or report inappropriate behaviour.

5   Model positive behaviour: Be a role model by demonstrating respectful and responsible online behaviour. Encourage empathy and understanding.

6   Report incidents: If your child experiences cyberbullying, promptly report it to the school and the relevant platform. Keep a record of any harmful messages or interactions.

7   Support and empower: Let your child know that they are not alone. Remind them that seeking help is a sign of strength, and that they can always turn to you, a teacher, or a school counsellor for assistance.

What we are doing:

- Addressing the issue directly with the pupils involved and taking appropriate actions.
- Organising workshops to educate pupils about the effects of cyberbullying and how to be responsible digital citizens.
- Fostering a positive and inclusive classroom environment through ongoing discussions and activities.

By working together, we can combat cyberbullying and ensure a safe and respectful digital space for all our pupils. If you have any concerns or suggestions, please don't hesitate to contact us. Thank you for your support in fostering a caring and empathetic community.

Sincerely,

[Teacher's Name]

[School Contact Information]

[School Logo]

Of course, you can generate similar letters to address any other problem behaviours in schools, such as poor attendance, vaping, or obvious signs of the lack of sleep.

Prompt: 'Write a parent information leaflet to help parents get children into a good sleep routine.'

Parent Information Leaflet: Establishing a Healthy Sleep Routine for Children

Dear Parents and Guardians,

We understand the importance of a good night's sleep in supporting your child's overall well-being and academic success. Developing a consistent sleep routine can significantly improve sleep quality and help your child wake up feeling refreshed and ready for the day ahead. This information leaflet aims to provide you with practical tips and guidance on creating a healthy sleep routine for your child.

1 Consistent bedtime and wake-up time: Set a regular bedtime and wake-up time for your child, even on weekends. Consistency helps regulate their internal body clock, making it easier to fall asleep and wake up.

2 Wind-down time: Create a calming pre-sleep routine to signal that it is time to relax. Activities like reading a book, listening to soothing music, or taking a warm bath can help your child transition from active play to restful sleep.

3 Limit screen time before bed: Reduce screen time at least an hour before bedtime. The blue light emitted by screens can interfere with the body's production of the sleep hormone, melatonin.

4 Comfortable sleep environment: Ensure your child's sleep space is comfortable and conducive to sleep. The room should be dark, quiet, and at a comfortable temperature.

5 Balanced meals and hydration: Avoid heavy or large meals close to bedtime. A light, balanced snack can be a good option. Also, encourage your child to hydrate during the day, but limit liquids before bedtime to avoid night time awakenings.

6 Limit caffeine intake: Keep an eye on your child's consumption of caffeinated beverages like fizzy and energy drinks, especially in the afternoon and evening.

7   Physical activity: Encourage physical activity during the day but avoid vigorous exercise close to bedtime. Gentle stretching or relaxation exercises can be a part of the bedtime routine.

8   Limit daytime naps: While short naps can be beneficial, lengthy daytime naps can interfere with night-time sleep. If your child naps, aim for a duration of about 20–30 minutes.

9   Communicate and collaborate: Discuss the importance of a sleep routine with your child and involve them in creating it. When they feel involved, they are more likely to stick to the routine.

10 Be patient: Establishing a new routine takes time. Be patient and understanding as your child adjusts to the changes.

Remember, a healthy sleep routine supports your child's overall health, academic performance, and emotional well-being. By prioritising sleep and providing a consistent routine, you are helping them build lifelong habits that contribute to their success.

If you have any questions or concerns, please feel free to reach out to the school nurse or counsellor.

Sincerely,

[Teacher's Name]

[School Contact Information]

[School Logo]

97. Planning Assessments

You can use AI to plan assessments very simply. I copied two 'time' benchmarks from the Scottish curriculum and asked AI to plan my assessment as follows: 'Can you plan me an assessment on the following benchmarks: "Reads and records time in both 12 hour and 24 hour notation and converts between the two. Knows the relationships between commonly used units of time and carries out simple conversion calculations, for example, changes 1¾ hours into minutes"?'[10]

Time Conversion and Notation

Objective: The objective of this assessment is to evaluate the pupil's ability to read and record time in both 12-hour and 24-hour notation, as well as their proficiency in converting between the two notations. Additionally, the assessment aims to assess the pupil's understanding of the relationships between commonly used units of time and their ability to carry out simple conversion calculations.

Assessment tasks:

1 Time notation identification (10 marks):
   - Provide the pupil with a series of time notations, including both 12-hour and 24-hour formats.
   - Ask the pupil to identify and record the time represented by each notation.

   Award 1 mark for each correct identification.

2 Time conversion (15 marks):
   - Present the pupil with a set of conversion problems involving both hours and minutes.
   - Ask the pupil to convert the given time from one unit to another (e.g. hours to minutes or minutes to hours).
   - Include a mix of whole numbers and fractions to assess the pupil's ability to handle different types of conversion calculations.

   Award 1 mark for each correct conversion.

10 Education Scotland, *Benchmarks: Second Level. All Curriculum Areas* (March 2017), p. 16. Available at: https://education.gov.scot/media/qohhrla0/secondlevelbenchmarksallareas_.pdf.

3 Time conversion word problems (15 marks):

- Provide the pupil with a set of word problems that require time conversion.

- Each problem should involve a real-life scenario where the pupil needs to convert time from one unit to another. For example: 'Sarah spent 2 hours and 30 minutes watching a movie. How many minutes did she spend watching the movie in total?'

Award 1 mark for each correctly solved word problem.

4 Application of time conversion (10 marks):

- Present the pupil with a scenario where they need to convert time between 12-hour and 24-hour notation. For example: 'You have a flight departing at 8.45pm. What is the equivalent time in 24-hour notation?'

Award 1 mark for each correctly solved problem.

5 Reflection (5 marks):

- Ask the pupil to reflect on their learning experience during this assessment.

- Encourage them to identify any challenges they faced and strategies they used to overcome them.

Award marks based on the pupil's ability to provide thoughtful and insightful reflections.

Total Marks: 55

Note: Adjust the number of tasks and marks allocated to each task based on the time available for the assessment and the specific needs of your pupils.

If I want to make my life even easier and not have to generate the questions myself, I can simply enter, 'Can you provide me with questions for the above assessment?'

---

1   Time notation identification:
   - Identify the time represented by the following notation: 3.45pm.
   - What time does 18:30 represent?
   - Convert 9.20am into 24-hour notation.
   - Write the time represented by 14:15 in 12-hour notation.
   - What time does 7.55pm indicate?

2   Time conversion:
   - Convert 2 hours into minutes.
   - How many minutes are there in 4.5 hours?
   - Change 90 minutes into hours.
   - Convert 3.25 hours into minutes.
   - How many hours are there in 180 minutes?

3   Time conversion word problems:
   - John spent 2 hours and 45 minutes playing video games. How many minutes did he spend playing in total?
   - Sarah has a 1-hour-and-20-minute train ride. How many minutes is that?
   - Emma baked a cake for 45 minutes and then let it cool for 20 minutes. How long did it take in total?
   - Tom jogged for 1 hour and 15 minutes. How many minutes did he jog?
   - Lisa has a 2-hour-and-30-minute dance class. How many minutes is that?

4   Application of time conversion:
   - You have a meeting scheduled for 10.30am. What is the equivalent time in 24-hour notation?
   - Your flight departs at 19:45. What is the equivalent time in 12-hour notation?
   - Convert 5.20pm into 24-hour notation.
   - Write the time 23:15 in 12-hour notation.

- What is the 24-hour notation for 8am?

5 Reflection:

- What was the most challenging part of this assessment for you? How did you overcome it?

- Did you find any particular strategies helpful in converting between different time units? Explain.

- Reflect on a specific question or problem that you found interesting or engaging. Why did you find it interesting?

- Were there any misconceptions or difficulties you encountered during this assessment? How did you address them?

- How confident do you feel in your ability to read and convert time in different notations? Explain.

Finally, you can achieve differentiation in seconds by typing, 'Can you give me an easier/more challenging version of the above assessment?'

98. Class Newsletters

Class newsletters are important pieces of communication for parents, although they can be laborious to create. I spend a lot of time thinking about how to word things and triple-checking my spelling and grammar (it only takes one slight error from a teacher to end up plastered all over social media!). You can type something very unpolished into an AI app and let it compose a professional sounding letter for you in seconds!

For example, inputting, 'Draft a newsletter to tell parents that this term we will be learning about fractions in maths, genres in reading, learning to use persuasive techniques in writing, Christianity in RE, colour in art, and working on a school nativity' gives you:

Newsletter: Exciting Learning Ahead!

Dear Parents and Guardians,

We hope this message finds you well. As we dive into another term of learning and growth, we are thrilled to share the exciting curriculum that awaits our pupils. From mathematics to the arts, we have a range of enriching subjects lined up to captivate their minds and nurture their talents.

Mathematics: exploring fractions

Get ready for some mathematical marvels! This term, our young mathematicians will be diving into the world of fractions. From understanding the basics to exploring operations with fractions, our pupils will be building a solid foundation in this essential area of mathematics.

Reading adventures: exploring genres

In the realm of reading, we are embarking on a journey through various literary genres. From mysteries that intrigue to fantasies that transport, our pupils will be discovering the wonderful world of storytelling across different genres.

Writing workshop: mastering persuasive techniques

Our budding writers are in for a treat as we delve into the art of persuasive writing. Through engaging activities and discussions, pupils will learn how to employ persuasive techniques to convey their ideas effectively and convincingly.

RE: exploring Christianity

This term, our RE lessons will focus on Christianity. Pupils will gain insights into the beliefs, traditions, and values that shape this prominent faith, fostering a deeper understanding of cultural diversity and religious tolerance.

Artistic expressions: the magic of colour

In the art studio, a world of colours awaits! Pupils will experiment with different hues, tints, and shades to create vibrant and captivating artworks. Our art classes promise to be a canvas of creativity and imagination.

Special project: school nativity

As the holiday season draws near, we are excited to announce that our school nativity is already in the works! Pupils will have the opportunity to participate in bringing the heart-warming story to life, celebrating unity and the spirit of giving.

We are dedicated to providing a well-rounded education that sparks curiosity, fosters growth, and nurtures creativity in our pupils. If you have any questions, suggestions, or would like to get involved, please don't hesitate to reach out to us.

Thank you for your continued support and partnership as we guide our pupils towards a successful and inspiring term ahead.

Warm regards,

[Teacher's Name]

[School Contact Information]

[School Logo]

99. Writing Pupil Learning Evaluations

Writing evaluative comments after a block of learning can be a time-intensive endeavour, often involving considerable time spent contemplating how to phrase statements appropriately. However, AI can streamline this process, producing a plethora of well-constructed alternatives that you can simply copy and paste. All you need to do is request differentiated evaluative comments focused on the benchmark you are assessing.

For example, 'Provide differentiated evaluative comments on pupil learning on the following benchmark: "Records amounts accurately in different ways using the correct notation, for example, 149p = £1.49 and 7p = £0.07." '[11]

Advanced level:

- Exemplary accuracy: Demonstrates exceptional accuracy in recording amounts using various notations. The ability to convert between different representations, such as 149p to £1.49 and 7p to £0.07, is consistently flawless.

- Thorough understanding: Clearly comprehends the relationship between pence and pounds, showcasing an in-depth understanding of decimal notation and its application in real-life contexts.

- Effortless adaptability: Skilfully adapts to different forms of notation, showcasing a high level of comfort and fluency in manipulating numerical values. This fluency extends to various currency-related scenarios.

Proficient level:

- Accurate conversion: Accurately records amounts using different notations, such as 149p = £1.49 and 7p = £0.07, with minor errors that do not significantly impact the overall understanding.

- Solid grasp: Demonstrates a solid grasp of the concept of converting between pence and pounds, although occasional errors may arise in complex scenarios.

11 Education Scotland, *Benchmarks: Numeracy and Mathematics* (June 2017), p. 15. Available at: https://education. gov.scot/media/s5edgtvx/numeracyandmathematicsbenchmarks.pdf.

- Effective application: Effectively applies the correct notation in most instances, showcasing consistent competency in handling currency-related calculations.

Developing level:

- Basic accuracy: Displays basic accuracy in recording amounts using different notations, such as 149p = £1.49 and 7p = £0.07, although errors occasionally occur in notation or conversion.

- Emerging understanding: Shows an emerging understanding of the relationship between pence and pounds but may require additional guidance to apply the concept accurately and consistently.

- Improvement opportunities: There is potential for improvement in ensuring consistent application of the correct notation and refining the conversion process between pence and pounds.

Remember that these comments are meant to provide constructive feedback based on the pupil's current level of achievement. Always consider the individual progress, context, and any specific challenges each pupil may face when providing feedback on their learning.

Note: AI has generated the 'advanced', 'proficient' and 'developing' levels, so always remember to adapt the text to the levels used in your school area.

100. Responding to World Events

When traumatic and frightening events take place in the world, parents can often be at a loss to know how best to handle the topic. Some parents may prefer not to discuss issues (such as the outbreak of a war) with their child, but they will undoubtedly hear about it at school. This is yet another task where AI can lend its assistance.

For example, 'Write a parent information letter on how to reassure children about the war in Ukraine.'

Parent Information Letter: Reassuring Children About the Situation in Ukraine

Dear Parents and Guardians,

We understand that recent news about the situation in Ukraine might raise concerns and questions for both you and your children. In times like these, it is natural for children to have worries and uncertainties. As caregivers, your role is crucial in providing them with the comfort and reassurance they need. This letter aims to offer you guidance on how to discuss the situation with your children in an age-appropriate and reassuring manner.

1   Be open to questions: Encourage your child to ask questions and express their feelings. Let them know that it is okay to feel concerned, and that you are there to listen and provide answers.

2   Choose age-appropriate language: When discussing complex events, tailor your explanations to your child's age and level of understanding. Use simple and clear language, avoiding graphic or frightening details.

3   Provide context: Explain the situation in a factual and objective manner. You can say something like, 'There is a situation happening far away in Ukraine, and people are working to find solutions.'

4   Focus on safety: Reassure your child that their safety is a priority and that the events are not affecting their immediate surroundings.

5   Limit exposure to media: While it is important to stay informed, constant exposure to news coverage can increase anxiety. Monitor your child's exposure to news and choose family-friendly news sources.

6   Share stories of resilience: Discuss examples of people coming together and helping one another during difficult times. Highlight stories of resilience and positive actions.

7   Maintain routines: Sticking to daily routines provides a sense of stability and predictability for children. Continue with regular activities and rituals that bring comfort.

8   Encourage expression: Allow your child to express their feelings through art, writing, or talking. Creative outlets can help them process their emotions.

9   Offer comfort: Physical comfort, such as hugs or spending quality time together, can provide a sense of security for children.

10 Monitor changes in behaviour: Keep an eye out for changes in your child's behaviour, sleep patterns, or school performance. If you notice significant shifts, consider seeking support from a school counsellor or mental health professional.

Remember, your support and presence make a significant difference in helping your child navigate challenging situations. By addressing their concerns openly and providing a safe space for them to express their feelings, you are helping them develop resilience and coping skills that will serve them well in the future.

If you have any concerns or questions, please don't hesitate to reach out to the school or your child's teacher.

Sincerely,

[Teacher's Name]

[School Contact Information]

[School Logo]

101. Prioritising Personal Health with AI

For me, the most significant advantage of AI is that, by alleviating some of the workload, it can improve teachers' health and quality of life. There are numerous ways to use AI to benefit your health and well-being outside of work too. For example, if you wanted to take up running, AI can help!

Prompt: 'Can you give me a couch to 5K running schedule?'

Here is a sample couch to 5K training schedule. This programme is designed to help beginners gradually build up their running endurance over a span of nine weeks, leading them to complete a five kilometre (3.1 mile) run. Remember to consult with a healthcare professional before starting any new exercise programme.

Week 1:
- Day 1: Run 60 seconds, walk 90 seconds (repeat for 20 minutes)
- Day 2: Run 60 seconds, walk 90 seconds (repeat for 20 minutes)
- Day 3: Run 60 seconds, walk 90 seconds (repeat for 20 minutes)

Week 2:
- Day 1: Run 90 seconds, walk 2 minutes (repeat for 20 minutes)
- Day 2: Run 90 seconds, walk 2 minutes (repeat for 20 minutes)
- Day 3: Run 90 seconds, walk 2 minutes (repeat for 20 minutes)

Week 3:
- Day 1: Run 90 seconds, walk 90 seconds, run 3 minutes, walk 3 minutes (repeat for 20 minutes)
- Day 2: Run 90 seconds, walk 90 seconds, run 3 minutes, walk 3 minutes (repeat for 20 minutes)
- Day 3: Run 90 seconds, walk 90 seconds, run 3 minutes, walk 3 minutes (repeat for 20 minutes)

Week 4:
- Day 1: Run 3 minutes, walk 90 seconds, run 5 minutes, walk 2.5 minutes (repeat for 25 minutes)

- Day 2: Run 3 minutes, walk 90 seconds, run 5 minutes, walk 2.5 minutes (repeat for 25 minutes)
- Day 3: Run 3 minutes, walk 90 seconds, run 5 minutes, walk 2.5 minutes (repeat for 25 minutes)

Week 5:

- Day 1: Run 5 minutes, walk 3 minutes, run 5 minutes, walk 3 minutes (repeat for 30 minutes)
- Day 2: Run 8 minutes, walk 5 minutes, run 8 minutes, walk 5 minutes (repeat for 35 minutes)
- Day 3: Run 20 minutes

Week 6:

- Day 1: Run 5 minutes, walk 3 minutes, run 8 minutes, walk 3 minutes, run 5 minutes (repeat for 32 minutes)
- Day 2: Run 10 minutes, walk 3 minutes, run 10 minutes (repeat for 26 minutes)
- Day 3: Run 22 minutes

Week 7:

- Day 1: Run 25 minutes
- Day 2: Run 28 minutes
- Day 3: Run 30 minutes

Week 8:

- Day 1: Run 28 minutes
- Day 2: Run 30 minutes
- Day 3: Run 30 minutes

Week 9:

- Day 1: Run 30 minutes
- Day 2: Run 30 minutes
- Day 3: Run a full 5K (3.1 miles)!

Remember to warm up before each run, cool down afterwards, and stay hydrated. Listen to your body and, if needed, repeat a week if you feel you need more time to build your endurance. Enjoy your running journey!

Conclusion

I appreciate that there are a number of ethical concerns around generative AI.

As we have seen, AI has the potential to amplify bias and discrimination. It tends to default to a Eurocentric perspective on history – for example, neglecting the essential role played by the Indian army in defeating the Nazis (unless explicitly prompted). It displays cognitive bias in respect of gender, sexuality, and ethnicity – for example, preferencing male names when asked for a list of footballers.

AI gathers information from various online resources and there is no guarantee of its accuracy. Furthermore, there is the possibility that malicious actors could use it to disseminate convincing-sounding misinformation to manipulate public opinion and potentially influence our democratic processes.

Typically, AI doesn't reference the information it generates, which means you can never be entirely certain that you haven't unintentionally plagiarised someone else's work. Likewise, although AI is capable of reproducing existing ideas, it may struggle to produce truly original thoughts.

When it comes to data gathering and privacy, as with social media platforms, a substantial amount of power and wealth is being concentrated in the hands of a very small number of individuals and corporations, essentially creating an oligarchy. Meanwhile, we currently lack the legal frameworks to address the protection of intellectual property rights.

As AI begins to pervade our lives, will it inhibit human connection and cause harm, or, with platforms like ChatGPT offering 'therapeutic' conversations, will this lead to a less stressful world? Will more advanced AI be an equaliser for neurodiverse pupils (and staff) or those with learning difficulties, or will it leave some pupils further behind?

While welcoming AI into the classroom, we must remain mindful of its limitations. Our commitment to inclusive and diverse education must remain at the forefront as we leverage AI in our classrooms. It is vital that we work to address biases and enrich the content we offer to our pupils.

Whatever your views on AI (and you are likely to be open to it if you are reading this book), it is here now, and there is no denying that it is going to change the way we learn and work. In my opinion, we may as well embrace AI and take advantage of what it has to offer. For too long, excessive workload has left many educators burned out and exhausted. This has been exacerbated by the increasing challenges of the profession, especially in the wake of COVID-19. This is where AI can step in as a transformative ally.

I remember a time when the internet and social media were shiny novelties that were met with scepticism and uncertainty. There are well-documented harms associated with social media, particularly for young people, such as addiction, low self-esteem, mental illness, exposure to harmful content, and the potential to be groomed, exploited, or radicalised by unscrupulous influencers. The parallels with AI are obvious. But, just as the internet reshaped communication and the dissemination of information, so AI has the capacity to reshape education, making it more accessible, personalised, and effective.

Throughout this book, we have delved into the myriad ways that AI can lighten our load and enhance our classrooms. The journey has been one of exploration and adaptation. As we conclude, it is clear that embracing AI doesn't mean forsaking our values or our role as educators. Instead, it can enable us to reclaim precious time and mental energy, allowing us to connect with our pupils more meaningfully, to craft imaginative lessons, and to cultivate the intellectual and emotional growth of those in our care.

We stand at the threshold of a new technological revolution. This is a pivotal moment. By adopting AI thoughtfully and wisely, we can shape the future of education to empower educators and learners alike.

Index of Subject Areas

Love Teaching, Keep Teaching

The essential guide to improving wellbeing at all levels in schools

Peter Radford

ISBN: 9781785835032

"A must-read for anyone who wants to delve into what makes teaching and learning tick."

Mick Waters, Professor of Education, University of Wolverhampton

Love Teaching, Keep Teaching is a practical guide to staying well in a high-pressure profession.

In the midst of a recruitment crisis and a massive exodus of teachers from our schools, now is the time for some joined-up thinking about teacher wellbeing and mental health.

Offering insightful advice and practical strategies, Peter invites you to think differently about the way education is 'done' and how you can keep doing the job you love without sacrificing your health and wellbeing.

Love Teaching, Keep Teaching paints a picture of a truly 'healthy school' as being one in which the value of each staff member and student is fundamental to everything we do. It also shares a fresh perspective on school leadership, encouraging leaders to rethink common practices and to explore the rewards and benefits of employing a people-focused approach.

Suitable for teachers and school leaders in both primary and secondary settings.

Teach Like You Imagined It
Finding the right balance
Kevin Lister

ISBN: 9781785834004

"Provides plenty to think about when it comes to refining our practice.."

Mary Myatt, adviser, speaker and author of
The Curriculum: From Gallimaufry to Coherence

Teach Like You Imagined It shares a wealth of tools, ideas and encouragement to help teachers manage the conflicting pressures of teaching and become the educators they imagined.

Teaching is an incredible profession, but it also comes with a potentially toxic workload. You do not have to put up with burn-out, however – and one way to avoid it is to return to how you imagined teaching to be in the first place.

Before you became a teacher, you pictured yourself as a teacher; in your imagination you almost certainly saw yourself as happy, efficient and able to manage your work–life balance effectively. Yet chances are that the reality of teaching is a little different, and it is this disconnect that can give rise to stress, anxiety and frustration.

But what if you could use simple strategies to get a handle on your schedule and take control of your workload?

Covering lesson planning, behaviour management, the streamlining of marking and getting the best out of CPD, Kevin Lister has drawn on his background in engineering to fill this book with trusted techniques and savvy suggestions to help you maximise your productivity and teach like you imagined it.

Suitable for both new and experienced teachers looking to boost their day-to-day efficiency and find the right balance.

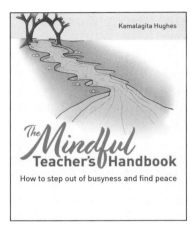

The Mindful Teacher's Handbook

How to step out of busyness and find peace

Kamalagita Hughes

ISBN: 9781785836428

"Gives you very practical ideas – both during routine and high-stress times."

Professor Rebecca Crane, PhD, Director, Centre for Mindfulness Research and Practice, Bangor University

The Mindful Teacher's Handbook is a practical and engaging resource to help everyone in schools bring mindfulness into their lives in a meaningful way. Mindfulness practice offers simple, straightforward strategies for finding peace and regaining perspective, and has a solid body of evidence that attests to its efficacy. In this book, Kamalagita Hughes provides a lively and engaging blend of top tips, research evidence, case studies, guided meditations and suggested exercises for all – both for those new to mindfulness and for those who want to refresh their practice.

Providing a thorough, grounded understanding of mindfulness and its benefits for the school community, the book explores the links between well-being and education and sets out how improved staff and student well-being can cultivate a better teaching and learning environment for all. Kamalagita offers practical strategies that school staff can put into practice straight away – both for their own well-being and that of their pupils – including insightful case studies on how best to bring mindfulness to your school.

Suitable for teachers, teaching assistants and school leaders.

Download a FREE resource from this book to help you manage your stress here: